AQA STUDY GUIDE

GCSE 9–1

A CHRISTMAS CAROL

BY CHARLES DICKENS

SCHOLASTIC

Author Cindy Torn

Series Consultants Richard Durant and Cindy Torn

Reviewer Rob Pollard

Editorial team Rachel Morgan, Audrey Stokes,
Camilla Erskine, Lesley Densham, Anne Henwood,
Louise Titley

Typesetting Oxford Designers and Illustrators

Cover design Nicolle Thomas, Neil Salt and
Alessandro Minoggi

App development Hannah Barnett, Phil Crothers and
RAIOSOFT International Pvt Ltd

Acknowledgements

Illustration Jim Eldridge/Oxford Designers & Illustrators

Photographs page 16: inscription, Tony Baggett/
Shutterstock; pages 19 and 75: chains, valeo5/Shutterstock;
pages 20 and 70: vintage sign, chrisdorney/Shutterstock;
pages 52, 54 and 75: gravestone, Chantal de Bruijne/
Shutterstock; page 59: coal, anat chant/Shutterstock; shilling,
Ian Sanders/Alamy; invitation, Pagina/Shutterstock; pages 59
and 62: money box, taviphoto/Shutterstock; page 74: foggy
street, Unholy Vault Designs/Shutterstock; page 74: winter
scene, Unholy Vault Designs/Shutterstock; page 75: shillings,
Yaroslaff/Shutterstock; page 76: factory, Peter Cripps/
Shutterstock; page 78: Charles Dickens, Everett Historical/
Shutterstock; page 80: alley, duncan1890/iStock; page 90:
girl doing exam, Monkey Business Images/Shutterstock;
page 93: notepad and pen, TRINACRIA PHOTO/Shutterstock

Published in the UK by Scholastic Education, 2019
Scholastic Distribution Centre, Bosworth Avenue,
Tournament Fields, Warwick, CV34 6UQ
Scholastic Ireland, 89E Lagan Road, Dublin Industrial Estate,
Glasnevin, Dublin, D11 HP5F
SCHOLASTIC and associated logos are trademarks and/or
registered trademarks of Scholastic Inc.

SCHOLASTIC and associated logos are trademarks and/or
registered trademarks of Scholastic Inc.
www.scholastic.co.uk
© 2019 Scholastic
9 3 4 5 6 7 8 9 0 1 2

A CIP catalogue record for this book is available from the
British Library.
ISBN 978-1407-18265-0

Printed and bound by Leo Paper Products Ltd, China.

The book is made of materials from
well-managed, FSC®-certified forests
and other controlled sources.

Designed using Adobe InDesign

Every effort has been made to trace copyright holders for the
works reproduced in this book, and the publishers apologise
for any inadvertent omissions.

Note from the publisher:
Please use this product in conjunction with the official
specification and sample assessment materials. Ask your
teacher if you are unsure where to find them.

Contents

Check your answers on the free revision app or at www.scholastic.co.uk/gcse

How to use this book

This Study Guide is designed to help you prepare effectively for your AQA GCSE English literature exam question on *A Christmas Carol* (Paper 1, Section B).

The content has been organised in a sequence that builds confidence, and which will deepen your knowledge and understanding of the novella step by step. Therefore, it is best to work through this book in the order that it is presented.

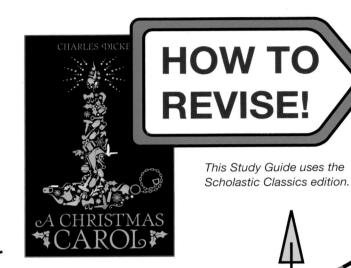

HOW TO REVISE!

This Study Guide uses the Scholastic Classics edition.

Know the plot

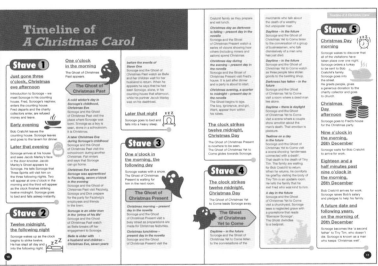

1 It is very important that you know the plot well: to be clear about what happens and in what order. The **timeline** on pages 10–11 provides a useful overview of the plot, highlighting key events.

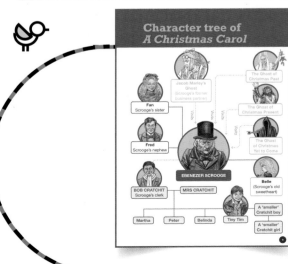

The **character tree** on page 9 introduces you to the main characters of the text.

The chronological section

2 The **chronological section** on pages 12–63 takes you through the novella scene by scene, providing plot summaries and pointing out important details. It is also designed to help you think about the structure of the novella.

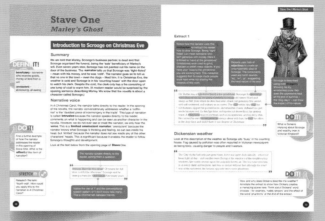

This section provides an in-depth exploration of themes or character development, drawing your attention to how Dickens' language choices reveal the novella's meaning.

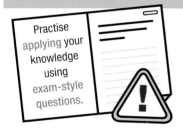

Practise applying your knowledge using exam-style questions.

The novella as a whole

3 The second half of the guide is retrospective: it helps you to look back over the whole novella through a number of relevant 'lenses': characters, themes, Dickens' language, forms and structural features.

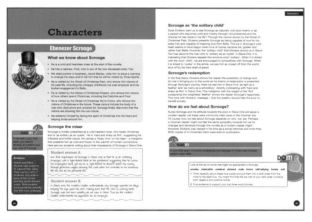

Doing well in your AQA Exam

Stick to the **TIME LIMITS** you will need to in the exam.

4 Finally, you will find an extended 'Doing well in your AQA exam' section which guides you through the process of understanding questions, and planning and writing answers.

Features of this guide

The best way to retain information is to take an active approach to revision.

Throughout this book, you will find lots of features that will make your revision an active, successful process.

SNAPIT!

Use the Snap it! feature in the revision app to take pictures of key concepts and information. Great for revision on the go!

DEFINEIT!

Explains the meaning of difficult words from the set texts.

Callouts Additional explanations of important points.

words shown in **purple bold** can be found in the glossary on pages 94–95

Find methods of relaxation that work for you throughout the revision period.

DOIT!

Regular exercise helps stimulate the brain and will help you relax.

Activities to embed your knowledge and understanding and prepare you for the exams.

NAILIT!

Succinct and vital tips on how to do well in your exam.

STRETCHIT!

Provides content that stretches you further.

REVIEW IT!

Helps you to consolidate and understand what you have learned before moving on.

Revise in pairs or small groups and deliver presentations on topics to each other.

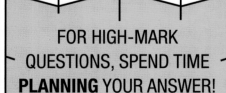

FOR HIGH-MARK QUESTIONS, SPEND TIME **PLANNING** YOUR ANSWER!

AQA exam-style question

AQA exam-style sample questions based on the extract shown are given on some pages. Use the sample mark scheme on page 86 to help you assess your responses. This will also help you understand what you could do to improve your response.

FREE REVISION APP

- The **free revision app** can be downloaded to your mobile phone (iOS and Android), making **on-the-go revision** easy.

- Use the revision calendar to help map out your revision in the lead-up to the exam.

- Complete multiple-choice questions and create your own SNAP IT! revision cards.

  www.scholastic.co.uk/gcse

Online answers and additional resources
All of the tasks in this book are designed to get you thinking and to consolidate your understanding through thought and application. Therefore, it is important to write your own answers before checking. Some questions include tables where you need to fill in your answer in the book. Other questions require you to use a separate piece of paper so that you can draft your response and work out the best way of answering.

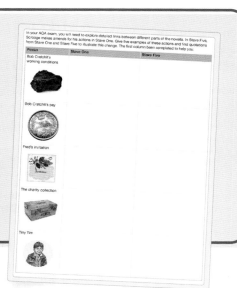

Get plenty of sleep, especially the night before an exam.

LOOK AFTER YOURSELF

Help your brain by looking after your whole body!

Once you have worked through a section, you can check your answers to Do it!, Stretch it!, Review it! and the exam practice sections on the app or at **www.scholastic.co.uk/gcse**.

Why study *A Christmas Carol*?

Even before you read *A Christmas Carol*, you may have heard the name Scrooge. Today, films are still being made of this novella or of modern reinventions of the characters and plots.

What is Dickens aiming to do with this novella? He wants to draw attention to the poor in society and the effects of poverty on those lives. He wants his readers to consider how they themselves may be part of society's problems through their ignorance of the needs of the poor.

It is a warning to society of what will happen if we don't shoulder our responsibilities. In our 21st-century world of food banks and rising poverty, we could do well to learn from Dickens' message.

A Christmas Carol in your AQA exam

A Christmas Carol is examined in Section B (the second half) of the first AQA GCSE English Literature exam, Paper 1: Shakespeare and 19th-century novel. Here is how it fits into the overall assessment framework:

Paper 1 Time: **1 hour 45 minutes**	Paper 2 Time: **2 hours 15 minutes**
Section A: Shakespeare	Section A: Modern prose or drama
Section B: 19th-century novel: *A Christmas Carol*	Section B: Poetry anthology
	Section C: Unseen poetry

There will be just **one question** on *A Christmas Carol* and you should not answer questions on any other 19th-century novel. Just answer the *A Christmas Carol* question. You should spend **50 minutes** planning and writing your answer to the question. There are 30 marks available for the 19th-century novel question.

The 19th-century novel question will come with a short extract from the novella printed on the exam paper. You will find the question straight after the extract. The question will focus on character and/or theme. You must answer the question in relation to the extract and to relevant other parts of the novella that you have chosen.

A character tree

The 'character tree' on page 9 should help you to fix in your mind the names of the characters, their relationships and who did what to whom.

Timeline of *A Christmas Carol*

The timeline on pages 10–11 provides a visual overview of the plot, highlighting key events which take place over the course of the novella. It will also help you to think about the structure of the novella.

NAILIT!

- Keep a close watch on the time in your exam. Don't spend more than 50 minutes on the *A Christmas Carol* question or you will have less time to write your answer to the Shakespeare question in Section A.

- Take special care over spelling, punctuation and grammar as there are four extra marks available for these.

Character tree of *A Christmas Carol*

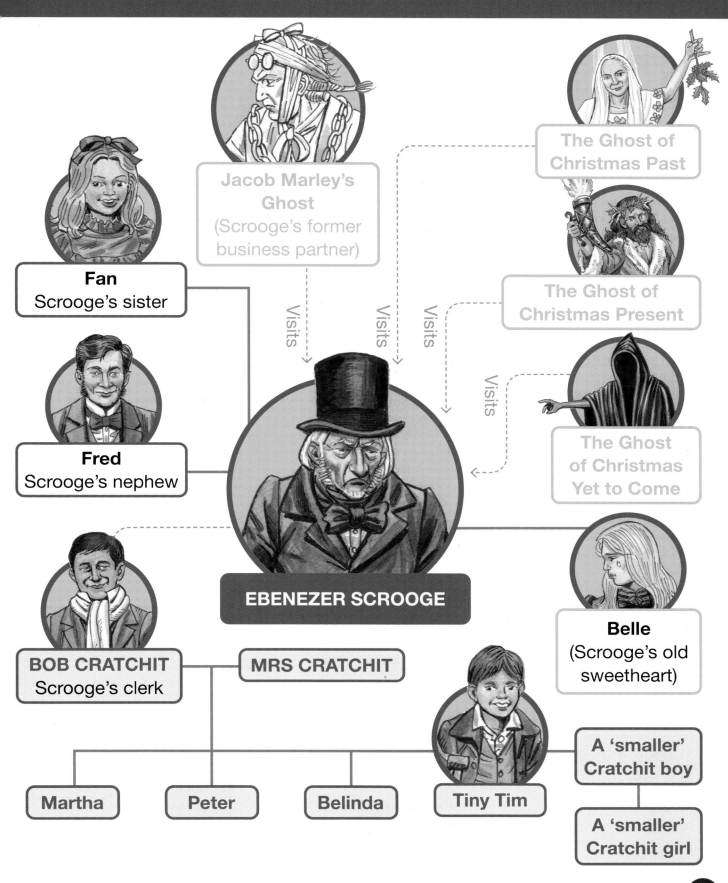

Jacob Marley's Ghost (Scrooge's former business partner)

The Ghost of Christmas Past

The Ghost of Christmas Present

Fan
Scrooge's sister

Fred
Scrooge's nephew

Visits

Visits

Visits

Visits

The Ghost of Christmas Yet to Come

EBENEZER SCROOGE

BOB CRATCHIT
Scrooge's clerk

MRS CRATCHIT

Belle
(Scrooge's old sweetheart)

A 'smaller' Cratchit boy

Martha

Peter

Belinda

Tiny Tim

A 'smaller' Cratchit girl

Timeline of *A Christmas Carol*

Stave 1

Just gone three o'clock, Christmas Eve afternoon

Introduction to Scrooge – we meet Scrooge in his counting house. Fred, Scrooge's nephew, enters the counting house. Fred departs and the charity collectors enter, are refused money and leave.

Early evening

Bob Cratchit leaves the counting house. Scrooge leaves and goes to the tavern for dinner.

Later that evening

Scrooge arrives at his house and sees Jacob Marley's face in the door-knocker. Jacob Marley's Ghost appears to Scrooge. He tells Scrooge that Three Spirits will visit him on the three following nights. Two will appear at one o'clock in the morning and the third will appear as the clock finishes striking twelve midnight. Scrooge goes to bed and falls asleep instantly.

Stave 2

Twelve midnight, the following night

Scrooge wakes up as the clock begins to strike twelve. He has slept all day and into the following night.

One o'clock in the morning

The Ghost of Christmas Past appears.

The Ghost of Christmas Past

A cold winter's day in Scrooge's childhood, Christmas Eve
Scrooge and the Ghost of Christmas Past visit the place where Scrooge was born. Scrooge as a boy is seen, alone in a schoolroom. It is Christmas.

A later Christmas Eve during Scrooge's childhood
Scrooge and the Ghost of Christmas Past visit the schoolroom during another Christmas. Fan enters and says that Scrooge can go home.

Christmas Eve when Scrooge was apprenticed to Fezziwig, seven o'clock in the evening
Scrooge and the Ghost of Christmas Past visit Fezziwig. Scrooge and Dick prepare for the party for Fezziwig's employees and friends in the town.

Scrooge is an older man in the 'prime of his life'
Scrooge and the Ghost of Christmas Past watch as Belle breaks off her engagement to Scrooge.

Belle is older with a husband and children – Christmas Eve, seven years

before the events of Stave One
Scrooge and the Ghost of Christmas Past watch as Belle and her children wait for her husband to return. When he appears he says that he had seen Scrooge, alone, in his counting house that afternoon, while his partner Jacob Marley was on his deathbed.

Later that night

Scrooge goes to bed and falls into a heavy sleep.

Stave 3

One o'clock in the morning, the following night

Scrooge wakes with a snore. The Ghost of Christmas Present is waiting for him in the next room.

The Ghost of Christmas Present

Christmas morning – present day in the novella
Scrooge and the Ghost of Christmas Present visit a busy street as preparations are made for Christmas festivities.

Christmas dinnertime – present day in the novella
Scrooge and the Ghost of Christmas Present visit the

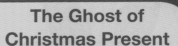

Cratchit family as they prepare and eat Christmas dinner.

Christmas day as darkness is falling – present day in the novella
Scrooge and the Ghost of Christmas Present watch a series of visions showing how others (including miners and sailors) spend Christmas.

Christmas evening – present day in the novella
Scrooge and the Ghost of Christmas Present visit Fred's house. It is just after dinner and a party is about to start.

Christmas night, a quarter to midnight – present day in the novella
The Ghost begins to age. The boy, Ignorance, and girl, Want, appear from within his robes.

The clock strikes twelve midnight

The Ghost of Christmas Present is nowhere to be seen.
The Ghost of Christmas Yet to Come glides towards Scrooge.

Stave 4

The clock strikes twelve midnight

The Ghost of Christmas Yet to Come leads Scrooge away.

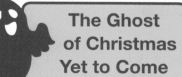

The Ghost of Christmas Yet to Come

Daytime – in the future
Scrooge and the Ghost of Christmas Yet to Come listen to the conversations of the merchants who talk about

the death of a wealthy but unpopular man.

Daytime – in the future
Scrooge and the Ghost of Christmas Yet to Come listen to the conversation of a group of businessmen, who talk dismissively of a man who has just died.

Daytime – in the future
Scrooge and the Ghost of Christmas Yet to Come watch as three people take stolen goods to the beetling shop.

Darkness has fallen – in the future
Scrooge and the Ghost of Christmas Yet to Come visit a room where a dead man lies alone.

Daytime – in the future, there is daylight
Scrooge and the Ghost of Christmas Yet to Come visit a scene where a couple show emotion about the man's death. That emotion is pleasure.

Teatime on a day in the future
Scrooge and the Ghost of Christmas Yet to Come visit a scene showing 'tenderness connected with a death'. That death is the death of Tiny Tim. The family are waiting for Bob Cratchit to return. When he returns, he comforts his grief by visiting the body of Tiny Tim in an upstairs room. He tells the family that he met Fred who was kind to him.

A different time in the future
Scrooge and the Ghost of Christmas Yet to Come visit a churchyard. Scrooge sees a neglected grave with a gravestone that reads 'Ebenezer Scrooge'. The Ghost dwindles to a bedpost.

Stave 5

Christmas Day morning

Scrooge wakes to discover that all of the visitations have taken place over one night. Scrooge orders a turkey to be sent to Bob Cratchit's family. Scrooge goes into the street. He greets people, gives a generous donation to the charity collector and goes to church.

Christmas Day afternoon

Scrooge goes to Fred's house for the Christmas party.

Nine o'clock in the morning, 26th December

Scrooge waits for Bob Cratchit to arrive for work.

Eighteen and a half minutes past nine in the morning, 26th December

Bob Cratchit arrives for work. Scrooge raises Bob's salary and pledges to help his family.

A future date and following years

Scrooge becomes like 'a second father' to Tiny Tim, who doesn't die. Scrooge is known as a man who keeps 'Christmas well'.

Stave One
Marley's Ghost

Introduction to Scrooge on Christmas Eve

Summary

We are told that Marley, Scrooge's business partner, is dead and that Scrooge organised the funeral, being the 'sole' beneficiary of Marley's will. Even seven years later, Scrooge has not painted out his name on the door of the business. The **narrator** tells us that Scrooge was 'tight-fisted' – mean with his money, and he was 'cold'. The narrator goes on to tell us that no one in the town – even the dogs – liked him. It is Christmas Eve, the weather is cold and Scrooge is in his 'counting house' with the door open to watch his clerk. Despite the cold, the clerk only has a fire consisting of one lump of coal to warm him. (A modern reader would be surprised by the opening sentence describing Marley. We know that the novella is about a character called Scrooge.)

Narrative voice

In *A Christmas Carol*, the narrator talks directly to the reader. In the opening of the novella, the narrator conversationally addresses whether a 'coffin-nail' is the 'deadest piece of ironmongery in the trade'. This type of narration is called **intrusive** because the narrator speaks directly to the reader, comments on what is happening and can be seen as another character in the novella. However, we do not ever see or meet the narrator; we only hear the **voice**. This is a **limited omniscient narrator**: 'omniscient' because the narrator knows what Scrooge is thinking and feeling, so can see inside his head, but 'limited' because the narrator does not see inside any of the other characters' heads. This is significant because it enables the reader to follow Scrooge's thoughts and development.

Look at the text below from the opening page of **Stave** One:

> The narrator speaks directly to the reader, asking them a question.

> " Scrooge knew he was dead? Of course he did. How could it be otherwise? Scrooge and he were partners for I don't know how many years. "

> Notice the use of 'I' and the conversational speech pattern of 'I don't know how many…' This is informal talk between friends.

 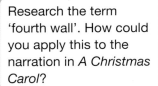

Extract 1

Notice how the narrator uses this **metaphor** to instruct the reader how to view Scrooge. Being 'tight-fisted' can mean someone who isn't generous with money. Here it is linked to 'hand at the grindstone'. Grindstones were used to grind, sharpen or polish metal objects. If you have your 'nose to the grindstone', you are working hard. This metaphor suggests that Scrooge made people work hard while not sharing the rewards of this work.

Dickens uses lists of **adjectives** to create an unsympathetic view of Scrooge. The consonants used are harsh sounds: 'sq', 'wr', 'gr', suggesting the hard nature of his soul.

Scrooge is described using cold **imagery**, showing his icy, emotionless core. Not even the oppressive heat of the end of summer – the 'dog-days' – can thaw the impact of his nature.

> Oh! But he was a tight-fisted hand at the grindstone, Scrooge! A squeezing, wrenching, grasping, scraping, clutching, covetous old sinner! Hard and sharp as flint, from which no steel had ever struck out generous fire; secret, and self-contained, and solitary as an oyster. The cold within him froze his
> 5 old features, nipped his pointed nose, shrivelled his cheek, stiffened his gait; made his eyes red, his thin lips blue; and spoke out shrewdly in his grating voice. A frosty rime was on his head, and on his eyebrows, and his wiry chin. He carried his own low temperature always about with him; he iced his office in the dog-days; and didn't thaw it one degree at Christmas.

Dickensian weather

Look at this description of the weather as Scrooge sits 'busy' in his counting house. Fog caused by pollution was often reported in Victorian newspapers as being toxic, causing danger to people and livestock.

> The City clocks had only just gone three, but it was quite dark already – it had not been light all day – and candles were flaring at the windows of the neighbouring windows, like ruddy smears upon the palpable brown air. The fog came pouring in at every chink and keyhole, and was so dense without, that although the court
> 5 was of the narrowest, the houses opposite were mere phantoms.

What is Dickens implying about Scrooge and wealthy men in Victorian England?

How and why does Dickens describe the weather? Annotate the extract to show how Dickens creates a menacing scene here. Think about Dickens' word choices – for example, 'ruddy smears' and the effect of the word 'phantoms' at the end of the extract.

The arrival of Fred

Summary

Into the gloom and cold of Scrooge's counting house suddenly bursts Fred, Scrooge's nephew. Fred wishes Scrooge a 'Merry Christmas', only to be met with Scrooge's views that Christmas belongs to 'a world of fools'. Fred defends the season, giving his definition of what is 'good', gaining applause from the clerk (Bob Cratchit) who then has to quickly stir the fire to cover his actions. Scrooge threatens to fire him if he makes another sound, before telling Fred that getting married for love is as foolish as Christmas. Fred invites his uncle to Christmas dinner the following day, then leaves cordially, wishing the clerk a 'Merry Christmas' as he goes. (Although many of the traditions we have at Christmas began in the Victorian era – and some were influenced by this novella – the feast at Christmas time had taken place throughout history.)

Presentation of Fred

Notice how Fred is presented as enthusiastic and cheerful as he enters the counting house – the antithesis (a contrast) to Scrooge. He does not react to Scrooge's opinions; instead he generously perseveres in inviting Scrooge to dinner. He has a 'cheerful' voice whereas Scrooge has a 'grating' voice; he is 'heated' whereas Scrooge is 'cold', and his opinions about money and Christmas are in direct contrast to Scrooge's opinions.

> 'If I could work my will,' said Scrooge indignantly, 'every idiot who goes about with "Merry Christmas" on his lips should be boiled with his own pudding, and buried with a stake of holly through his heart. He should!'

Notice here the contrast between Scrooge's opinion of Christmas and Fred's opinion of Christmas. Dickens uses humour with his exaggerated image of death by a stake of holly to signal to the reader that we should agree with Fred's opinion rather than Scrooge's opinion.

Look at what Fred has to say about 'good'. Scrooge has just introduced the idea that no 'good' – by which he means money – will come from Christmas. Fred responds that he has 'derived good' from many things 'by which I have not profited'.

Dickens' use of colour

Extract 1

Fred (Scrooge's nephew) enters the counting house. Dickens' **language choices** reinforce the implication that Fred's opinions are healthier than Scrooge's.

> Fred is a confident speaker, in a similar way to his uncle, Scrooge.

"

'A merry Christmas, Uncle! God save you!' cried a cheerful voice. It was the voice of Scrooge's nephew, who came upon him so quickly that this was the first intimation he had of his approach. 'Bah!' said Scrooge. 'Humbug!'

5   He had so heated himself with rapid walking in the fog and frost, this nephew of Scrooge's, that he was all in a glow; his face was ruddy and handsome; his eyes sparkled, and his breath smoked again…

…'Don't be angry, Uncle. Come! Dine with us tomorrow.' Scrooge said that he would see him ____. Yes, indeed he did. He

10 went the whole length of the expression, and said that he would see him in that extremity first.

"

> Fred's face is a healthy red colour. The fog has been a toxic 'brown'; Scrooge's eyes were 'red' suggesting illness and his lips were 'blue' with cold. Fred enters, bringing light – 'his eyes sparkled', and heat – 'he was all in a glow'.

AQA exam-style question

Starting with this extract, explore how Dickens presents attitudes towards Christmas in *A Christmas Carol*.

Write about:

- how Dickens presents attitudes towards Christmas in this extract

- how Dickens presents attitudes towards Christmas in the novella as a whole.

[30 marks]

STRETCH IT!

To gain the highest marks in your exam, you need to explore detailed links between different parts of the novella. Compare how Scrooge reacts towards Fred at this point in the novella and how he reacts to Fred in Stave Five. What is Dickens showing the reader with this contrast?

A student has written part of their response to this exam question.

Dickens demonstrates Fred's attitude towards Christmas through respect for the Christmas tradition of a family meal in spite of Scrooge's rude behaviour. His persistent insistence that Scrooge 'dine with [them] tomorrow,' suggests that he values Christmas. It could be argued that Dickens uses Fred's character to contrast with and highlight Scrooge's miserable existence, regardless of his wealth. Dickens is showing the reader that it is sharing time and a meal with a loving family that is important within society, and all of Scrooge's money cannot buy the happiness gained by being with family. Dickens is criticising Victorian society here by suggesting that people like Scrooge need to share their wealth to help others. This is a message that is still relevant today.

DO IT!

Where does the student:

- answer the question?

- provide **evidence**?

- explain how the evidence links to the question, including contextual awareness?

The charity collectors

Summary

As the clerk shows Fred out, he lets in two 'portly gentlemen' who arrive to collect charitable donations for the poor. Scrooge expresses his support for the workhouses, prisons and the Poor Law. He refuses to make a donation because he 'can't afford to make idle people merry' and the charity collectors leave. A carol singer who arrives at Scrooge's door is chased away, fleeing 'in terror'.

Scrooge shuts up the counting house, reluctantly allows the clerk a day off for Christmas Day, but insists that he arrive early the day after that. The clerk is seen heading home 'as hard as he could pelt' to play 'blind-man's buff' with his family.

Rich and poor

This section in the novella reveals Dickens' message regarding the injustice faced by the poor. The gap between rich and poor was massive in Victorian Britain at this time, and there was growing concern amongst some wealthy people that there was not enough being done to support those living in poverty. The 'portly' charity collectors represent these people. The clerk (Bob Cratchit) represents workers who are exploited by wealthy employers.

Victorian attitudes to poverty and the poor

Extract 1

DO IT!

How do the charity collectors react to Scrooge's **point of view**?' What is Dickens showing the reader? Write a paragraph using evidence to support your views.

Prisons were used for people who were unable to pay their debts as well as those who had committed criminal offences.

> 'Are there no prisons?' asked Scrooge.
> 'Plenty of prisons,' said the gentleman, laying down the pen again.
> 'And the union workhouses?' demanded
> 5 Scrooge. 'Are they still in operation?'
> 'They are. Still,' returned the gentleman, 'I wish I could say they were not.'
> 'The Treadmill and the Poor Law are in full vigour, then?' said Scrooge.
> 10 'Both very busy, sir.'
> 'Oh! I was afraid, from what you said at first, that something had occurred to stop them in their useful course,' said Scrooge. 'I am very glad to hear it.'

In 1834 the Poor Law Amendment Act was passed, establishing workhouses. If the poor needed help or aid, they would have to enter a workhouse to get it. Dickens campaigned against this law.

Debtors' prisons were workhouses where prisoners completed hard and repetitive tasks to help them contemplate their crime. Punishments included the Treadmill where prisoners ground grain or pumped water for up to eight hours a day. Wages were used to pay off debts. The poor feared workhouses, seeing them as a last desperate resort.

Extract 2

The charity collectors ask Scrooge to make a donation to help the poor.

> 'I wish to be left alone,' said Scrooge. 'Since you ask me what I wish, gentlemen, that is my answer. I don't make merry myself at Christmas, and I can't afford to make idle people merry. I help support the establishments I have mentioned – they
> 5 cost enough; and those who are badly off must go there.'
> 'Many can't go there; and many would rather die.'
> 'If they would rather die,' said Scrooge, 'they had better do it, and decrease the surplus population.'

Scrooge voices a belief that was commonly held at the time – that people were poor because they were lazy or because of their own irresponsible behaviour. This is a belief that is still held by some people within our society.

Scrooge shows his contempt and lack of compassion for the poor by his language, seeing death or suicide as a means of decreasing 'the surplus population'. The adjective 'surplus' is the language of business: people are disposable commodities.

Bob Cratchit, the clerk

We meet the clerk for the second time here. It is the end of the day on Christmas Eve and Scrooge is unhappy that Cratchit will have the whole of the next day off. The clerk's respectful language, 'if quite convenient, sir' in the face of Scrooge's ill-temper, shows his lowly status and lack of power. Cratchit represents working-class people exploited by their employers. Scrooge holds the power and Dickens makes sure the reader understands this. The clerk's joy as he rushes home to his family contrasts with Scrooge's solitary life.

AQA exam-style question

Starting with these extracts, explore how Dickens presents attitudes to poverty and the poor in *A Christmas Carol*. Write about:

- how Dickens presents attitudes towards poverty and the poor in these extracts
- how Dickens presents attitudes towards poverty and the poor in the novella as a whole.

[30 marks]

NAILIT!

Your AQA exam question stem is always '*how* Dickens *presents*...'

- 'how' is about the methods Dickens uses
- 'presents' is not just about *what* he is saying about the topic, but also his attitude towards that topic, and how he wants *us* to respond to it.

The Ghost of Jacob Marley

Summary

Scrooge heads for his dinner before returning home. As he looks at the door-knocker, he sees the face of his dead business partner, Jacob Marley. Scrooge is unnerved, but dismisses it once he gets inside the house. A 'disused' bell begins to ring loudly, joined by every other bell in the house. As the noise of footsteps approaches Scrooge, Jacob Marley's Ghost appears, transparent and wrapped in chains. He tells Scrooge that he forged his chains 'in life'. Marley warns Scrooge that the torment that Marley is experiencing will be Scrooge's fate. (Dickens uses Christian images of purgatory as Marley cannot escape his punishment.) Marley says that Three Spirits will appear over the next three nights and without those visits Scrooge cannot escape Marley's fate.

Marley walks backwards towards a window, which magically opens to reveal a host of phantoms, all wearing chains like Marley's chains. Scrooge closes the window and falls asleep.

This section has moments of comedy (Scrooge inviting the Ghost to sit down) and moments of **Gothic** horror (the macabre nature of the jaw dropping to Marley's chest).

'I wear the chain I forged in life': Marley's chains

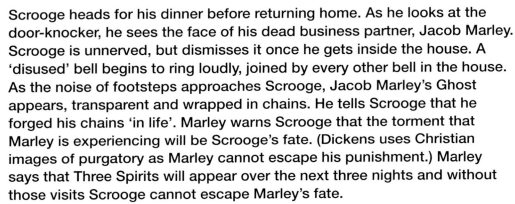

> "The chain he drew was clasped about his middle. It was long, and wound about him like a tail; and it was made…of cash boxes, keys,
> 5 padlocks, ledgers, deeds, and heavy purses wrought in steel."

Marley's chains represent the things that preoccupied him during his life. They symbolise his life bound up in pursuit of wealth.

The items are linked with the world of business and making money: a ledger would record business transactions; cashboxes would store money.

Steel is a hard, grey metal known for its strength. Marley cannot escape the guilt of not helping people when he had the opportunity during his life. Scrooge has had an additional seven years (since Marley died) of not helping people when he had the chance.

Gothic horror

Gothic horror (see also page 83) was very fashionable in the Victorian era. This genre of literature, characterised by features chosen to create fear, contained some of the following elements:

- a hero
- someone in need of rescue (usually a woman)
- supernatural beings or monsters
- a dark/gloomy **setting**, such as castles, old houses, ruined churches
- warnings, curses or prophecies
- high emotion or melodrama.

DOIT!

How does Dickens use elements of Gothic horror writing from Scrooge arriving home to the end of the Stave One and what is their effect?

Extract 1

The Ghost of Jacob Marley outlines one of Dickens' key messages within the novella: that our key purpose in life should be to help other people.

Here Dickens plays with the word 'business'.

Scrooge congratulates Marley on his role as a good man of business – meaning that he ran his company well (probably also suggesting that he made lots of money through his business).

'Business!' The Ghost's one-word declaration, coupled with the exclamation mark, shows the reader Marley's horrified reaction to what Scrooge has just said. The Ghost is reacting to 'business' and 'good' being linked together.

> 'But you were always a good man of business, Jacob,' faltered Scrooge, who now began to apply this to himself.
> 'Business!' cried the Ghost, wringing its
> 5 hands again. 'Mankind was my business. The common welfare was my business; charity, mercy, forbearance and benevolence were, all, my business. The dealings of my trade were but a drop of water in the comprehensive
> 10 ocean of my business!'

Marley tells Scrooge that 'business' (his life's work) should have been to help mankind. Instead he focused on making money. Notice that the qualities he lists are all virtues.

By showing the host of phantoms at the end of the stave, Dickens makes his message universal: this is a message for us all, not just one solitary man.

DEFINE IT!

benevolence – the quality of being kind-hearted and compassionate

charity – voluntarily giving help (often money) to people in need

forbearance – self-control and restraint

mercy – compassion or forgiveness

phantoms – ghosts

purgatory – a place of suffering where Catholics believe a person's soul goes after death, so they can be cleansed of evil acts carried out during their lifetime

Stave One and the novella structure

The characters within the novella have been introduced and set up in this opening stave. The **structure** of the rest of the novella will be framed around the visits from each of the Three Ghosts and the consequences of those visits.

DO IT!

1 Jacob Marley tells Scrooge that Three Ghosts will haunt him. Find **quotations** within this stave to illustrate when these hauntings will take place.

2 Within this section with the Ghost of Jacob Marley, what references to time do you notice?

STRETCH IT!

How and why does Dickens use the **theme** of time in this section of the novella? Write a paragraph to explain your ideas.

Theme and character essentials

Social responsibility

Dickens presents Scrooge's attitudes to the poor when he asks the charity collectors, 'Are there no workhouses?' Workhouses were places of severe hardship. Here Dickens highlights attitudes of wealthy people in Victorian society who believed that the poverty people faced was because of being lazy or unwilling to work. The phantoms Scrooge sees outside his window at the end of the stave allow Dickens to point out that Scrooge is not alone in his need for redemption.

Christmas

The title of the novella refers to a traditional Christmas song and the chapters are staves, which are parts of musical notation. Christmas is a Christian festival and is associated with generosity, joy, celebration and love for family and humanity. Scrooge is presented as turning his back on Christmas – and therefore on these qualities.

The narrator

The narrator comments on the action of the novella playfully in the opening of the stave. The voice addresses the reader directly: 'You will, therefore, permit me to repeat', and plays with the word 'sole' (soul) when talking of Scrooge and Marley's friendship: 'his sole friend and sole mourner'.

Scrooge

Scrooge is 'a tight-fisted hand at the grindstone' who is not influenced by any factors other than the pursuit of money and business: no 'heat' or 'cold'; no festive times of year; no understanding of love; no compassion for 'the poor and destitute'. The reader sees his tendency to try to be 'smart' when he is afraid and we understand that he is afraid to trust his senses because a 'little thing affects them'. This stave is vital when writing about the theme of redemption in the novella, for in it we see why Scrooge needs to begin his journey towards salvation.

Fred

As the antithesis to Scrooge, Fred represents the Christmas spirit, showing generosity and forgiveness to his ungrateful uncle. Fred tells Scrooge that, although Christmas has never 'put a scrap of gold or silver' in his pocket, Fred believes that 'it *has* done me good, and *will* do me good; and I say, God bless it!'

Jacob Marley's Ghost

Jacob Marley's Ghost is presented as a terrifying phantom, wrapped in chains, which he clanks 'hideously in the dead silence of the night'. These chains symbolise his motivations during his life – money and business. His friendship towards Scrooge is shown as he seeks to stop Scrooge facing the same 'Incessant torture of remorse' that he has endured for the past seven years. His message sets up the visitation of three further spirits, which also sets up the structure of the novella.

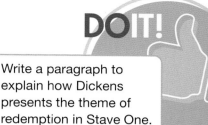

DO IT!

Write a paragraph to explain how Dickens presents the theme of redemption in Stave One.

REVIEW IT!

1   Why is the opening to Stave One surprising?

2   Why does Scrooge keep the door of his counting house open?

3   What does the metaphor 'dismal little cell' suggest?

4   Scrooge is described with cold images whereas Fred is described with images of heat. What is Dickens showing the reader here?

5   What is Scrooge's reaction to Fred's answer that he married for love?

6   How does Scrooge feel about the poor?

7   What does Scrooge see as his role in helping the welfare of the poor?

8   Look at these quotations about the weather. Match the quotation with the relevant language analysis.

'Meanwhile the fog and darkness thickened so'	Use of successive clauses builds the intensity and effect of cold. **Personification** suggests that cold distrusts humankind.
'as if its teeth were chattering in its frozen head'	The list of adjectives reveals the violent and menacing nature of cold.
'The water-plug being left in solitude, its overflowings suddenly congealed, and turned to misanthropic ice.'	The use of personification that is extended by a **simile** alarmingly describes the effects of the weather on a face.
'Piercing, searching, biting cold.'	Personification of the church conveys the extent and effect of cold.
'The owner of one scant young nose, gnawed and mumbled by the hungry cold as bones are gnawed by dogs, stooped down at Scrooge's keyhole'	The time connective and the verb suggest the weather is closing in and getting worse.

9   **"**
> It must have run there when it was a young house, playing at hide-and-seek with other houses and have forgotten the way out again.

"

What **technique** does Dickens use to describe his house? What is he suggesting in his use of this technique?

10   How does Scrooge react initially to the signs of the haunting by Marley's Ghost?

11   Marley's eyes are described as 'glazed'. What does this adjective suggest about them?

12   What are Marley's chains made of? What do they symbolise?

13   Marley's spirit is condemned to 'wander through the world'. What is he forced to witness during these wanderings?

14   Scrooge tells Marley, "You were always a good friend to me!" How does Marley show his friendship towards Scrooge in this section?

15   As Scrooge goes to the window, what does he see outside? What is Dickens' message to the reader here?

16   At the end of Stave One, Scrooge does not finish the word "Humbug!" What is Dickens suggesting here?

Stave Two
The First of the Three Spirits

The Ghost of Christmas Past

Summary

Scrooge wakes up and listens to the clock strike. Despite going to bed at past two o'clock in the morning, the clock strikes twelve. Scrooge thinks it is not possible to have slept through a whole day and 'far onto another night'. As the clock strikes one o'clock, a hand draws back the bed curtains. A strange, shifting figure stands beside the bed – sometimes appearing as a child and sometimes as an old man. The Spirit has a jet of 'bright clear' light from the top of its head and an 'extinguisher for a cap' under its arm. This is the Ghost of Christmas Past. The Ghost gives his reason for being there as Scrooge's 'welfare', as he takes Scrooge to an open country road. The city has vanished and it is a 'clear cold' day with snow on the ground.

Time

Dickens presents the supernatural nature of the visitation with this shift in time. Through this device, he is also able to resolve a possible difficulty with the structure of Three Ghosts/Spirits on successive nights and what Scrooge would do during each day.

Dickens and the weather

In this section, once again the reader is shown a world shrouded in fog and cold, suggesting the cold, isolating life that Scrooge is living and the fog of ignorance – both Scrooge's and society's ignorance – of the lives of the poor and needy.

Youth, age and memory

DO IT!

Write out this description and highlight:
- images of youth
- images to show age.

Why does Dickens present the Ghost of Christmas Past in this way?

> It was a strange figure – like a child: yet not so like a child as like an old man, viewed through some supernatural medium, which gave him the appearance of having receded from the view, and being diminished to a child's
> 5 proportions. Its hair, which hung about its neck and down its back, was white as if with age; and yet the face had not a wrinkle in it, and the tenderest bloom was on the skin.

Notice the unsettling description of this 'strange' figure. It is constantly shifting between childlike impressions and aged impressions.

Memory connects all stages of our lives. We have memories from our childhood and memories as we grow older. Sometimes, in order to see things clearly, we need to examine these memories. Dickens shows the reader how the light from this Ghost allows Scrooge to examine these memories.

Extract 1

Scrooge meets the Ghost of Christmas Past. The supernatural was a controversial topic in the 19th century. Many people believed in the supernatural and these elements were associated with the devil and evil. Notice how Dickens uses contrasts to show the Ghost of Christmas Past.

"

The arms were very long and muscular; the hands the same, as if its hold were of uncommon strength. Its legs and feet, most delicately formed, were, like those upper members, bare. It wore a tunic of the purest white, and round its waist was bound a

5 lustrous belt, the sheen of which was beautiful. It held a branch of fresh green holly in its hand; and, in singular contradiction of that wintry emblem, had its dress trimmed with summer flowers. But the strangest thing about it was, that from the crown of its head there sprung a bright clear jet of light, by which all this was

10 visible; and which was doubtless the occasion of its using, in its duller moments, a great extinguisher for a cap, which it now held under its arm.

Even this, though, when Scrooge looked at it with increasing steadiness, was *not* its strangest quality. For as its belt sparkled

15 and glittered now in one part and now in another, and what was light one instant, at another time was dark, so the figure itself fluctuated in its distinctness: being now a thing with one arm, now with one leg, now with twenty legs, now a pair of legs without a head, now a head without a body: of which dissolving

20 parts, no outline would be visible in the dense gloom wherein they melted away. And in the very wonder of this, it would be itself again; distinct and clear as ever.

"

Contrast between strength and delicacy represents memory.
Colour contrast of white and green represents innocence and maturity.
Contrast between seasonal flowers (winter and summer) represents time.
Contrasts between light and dark.
Contrasts and fluctuations of shape.
Contrasts in substance: dissolving then being distinct.

DO IT!

1 Look at the description of the Ghost of Christmas Past in extract 1. What does the Ghost's head look like? What is the function of this light?

2 How does Dickens present the Ghost of Christmas Past in extract 1?

STRETCH IT!

In your own words, explain what Dickens is suggesting about memory through his use of symbolism in his description of the Ghost of Christmas Past in extract 1. Comment on the effect on the intended reader.

The solitary child and Fan

Summary

The Ghost of Christmas Past takes Scrooge to the place where he grew up. Scrooge recognises places and people and he is glad to see these people. The Ghost shows Scrooge a 'solitary child' left in a schoolhouse. Scrooge weeps at this memory of his 'poor forgotten self'. Scrooge excitedly remembers the books that the boy is reading before remembering the carol singer who he had turned away from his door the previous evening.

The Ghost shows Scrooge another Christmas, where once again he is alone in a room. His younger sister, Fan, enters the room and tells him that he can go home. Scrooge and the Ghost discuss Fan's generous heart and they reveal that before she died she had one child – Fred.

Scrooge's past experiences

Within this section, Dickens shows the reader Scrooge's past experiences and how they have created the man that we meet in Stave One. However, Dickens also shows us Scrooge's happiness when he sees familiar landscapes and people. We also see how he filled his 'solitary' life with adventure stories and characters from books. He is able to weep and feel emotion for the 'solitary child' that he was. This enables him to consider that he should have been kinder to the carol singer the previous evening.

Cracks in the ice

> "
> The Spirit gazed on him mildly. Its gentle touch, though it had been light and instantaneous, appeared still present to the old man's sense of feeling. He was
> 5 conscious of a thousand odours floating in the air, each one connected with a thousand thoughts, and hopes, and joys, and cares long, long forgotten!
>
> 'Your lip is trembling,' said the Ghost.
> 10 'And what is that on your cheek?'
> "

The Ghost is presented as gentle. Notice Dickens, use of the **adverb** 'mildly' to show how the Ghost looks at Scrooge serenely and kindly.

At this point, Scrooge begins to experience sensations – a shift from his former oyster-like self.

Dickens lists these sensations to show the waves of feelings and sensations that Scrooge was experiencing.

The Ghost indicates that Scrooge is feeling emotion. Notice the Ghost doesn't say directly, 'You are crying', but instead asks a question, leaving it to Scrooge to recognise and name the emotion. However, Scrooge can only mutter and say that it is a "pimple".

DOIT!

1 How does Dickens present Scrooge's early life in this section?
2 What new behaviours do we see from Scrooge for the first time here?
3 How might this section change the reader's perception of Scrooge?

Extract 1

Scrooge sees a vision of himself as a child, left in school, at Christmas.

Dickens presents Fan using a term of endearment as a shortcut to show the close relationship she has with her brother.

Like Fred, Fan is shown as a force of joy and happiness. She is shown 'clapping her hands' and 'bending down to laugh'. This joyful noise contrasts with the silence of the counting house from Stave One.

> 'I have come to bring you home, dear brother!' said the child, clapping her tiny hands, and bending down to laugh. 'To bring you home, home, home!'
>
> 5 'Home, little Fan?' returned the boy.
> 'Yes!' said the child, brimful of glee. 'Home, for good and all. Home, for ever and ever. Father is so much kinder than he used to be, that home's like Heaven! He spoke so gently to me one dear
> 10 night when I was going to bed, that I was not afraid to ask him once more if you might come home; and he said Yes, you should; and sent me in a coach to bring you. And you're to be a man!' said the child, opening her eyes, 'and are never
> 15 to come back here; but first, we're to be together all the Christmas long, and have the merriest time in all the world.'

Mixed with the joyful 'glee' with which Fan gives Scrooge the news of his homecoming, there are dark suggestions regarding Scrooge's home life and his relationship with his father. Again, Dickens signals underlying reasons for Scrooge's behaviour in the opening stave. What is interesting is that, in his early years, that isolation was forced upon him, whereas as an adult he has chosen to isolate himself.

DO IT!

1 What is implied in this extract about Scrooge's father? Write a paragraph to explain your ideas.

2 What effect does watching the memory of Fan's appearance at the school have on Scrooge?

3 At the end of the stave, the Ghost reminds Scrooge that Fred is Fan's child.

   a Explain Scrooge's reaction to the prompting of the Ghost:
   'Scrooge seemed uneasy in his mind; and answered briefly, "Yes."'

   b How does this fit into the theme of redemption?

 STRETCH IT!

How does this extract with Fan help to change the reader's opinion of Scrooge at this point in the novella?

Fezziwig

Summary

The Ghost of Christmas Past goes to the warehouse where Scrooge was apprenticed to Fezziwig. Scrooge is now a young man. Fezziwig calls to his apprentices to prepare the warehouse for the Christmas party. Workers and the Fezziwig family gather to dance and eat. Scrooge enjoys the party as much as he did when he was younger. Scrooge and the Ghost listen to two apprentices praise Fezziwig, and Scrooge reflects on how an employer can make his workers happy or unhappy. Scrooge tells the Ghost that he wishes he could "say a word or two" to his clerk, Bob Cratchit.

Scrooge's joy at seeing his former boss is shown through the use of exclamations and the repetition of Fezziwig's name. Dickens uses a **charactonym** here to **imply** traits within Fezziwig, such as soft consonants 'f', 'zz', 'w' to suggest a warm personality.

> Scrooge cried in great excitement:
> 'Why it's old Fezziwig! Bless his heart, it's Fezziwig alive again!'
> Old Fezziwig laid down his pen, and looked up
> 5 at the clock, which pointed to the hour of seven.
> He rubbed hands; adjusted his capacious waistcoat; laughed all over himself, from his shoes to his organ of benevolence; and called out, in a comfortable, oily, rich, fat, jovial voice:
> 10 'Yo ho, there! Ebenezer! Dick!'

Dickens lists Fezziwig's actions to show his decisive manner: putting 'down his pen' signals that work is at an end for the day while the details of how he 'laughed', adjusted his waistcoat and called out in a richly descriptive **tone** of voice are sensual descriptions that create a character that is a **foil** to the 'cold' description of Scrooge.

DO IT!

STRETCH IT!

Look at the section where Fezziwig tells his apprentices that there will be "No more work tonight." Compare this to how Scrooge tells his clerk that the counting house was to be shut for the night: 'At length the hour of shutting up the counting house arrived. With an ill-will Scrooge... tacitly admitted the fact'

Look at the description of the party, from 'Clear away! There was nothing they wouldn't have cleared away...' to 'When the clock struck eleven, this domestic ball broke up.'

Find quotations to show descriptions of the following elements of the party:

- heat or warmth to symbolise companionship with friends and family

- food to symbolise plenty and the joy of sharing food with family

- music and dancing to symbolise celebration and happiness.

Extract 1

The adjective 'silly' shows the dismissive tone used by the Ghost. The Ghost uses language Scrooge would have used previously.

" 'A small matter,' said the Ghost, 'to make these silly folks so full of gratitude.'

'Small!' echoed Scrooge.

The Spirit signed to him to listen to the two apprentices, who were pouring out their hearts in praise of Fezziwig; and when he had done so, said:

5 'Why! Is it not? He has spent but a few pounds of your mortal money: three or four perhaps. Is that so much that he deserves this praise?'

'It isn't that,' said Scrooge, heated by the remark, and speaking unconsciously like his former, not his latter, self. 'It isn't that, Spirit. He has the power to render us happy or unhappy; to make our service light or

10 burdensome; a pleasure or a toil. Say that his power lies in words and looks; in things so slight and insignificant that it is impossible to add and count 'em up: what then? The happiness he gives is quite as great as if it cost a fortune.' "

The verb 'heated' suggests anger, indicating Scrooge's emotional response to these memories; the reader will also recognises that Scrooge is usually 'cold'.

Scrooge uses counting house language, but also learns the power a good employer can have to keep his workforce happy.

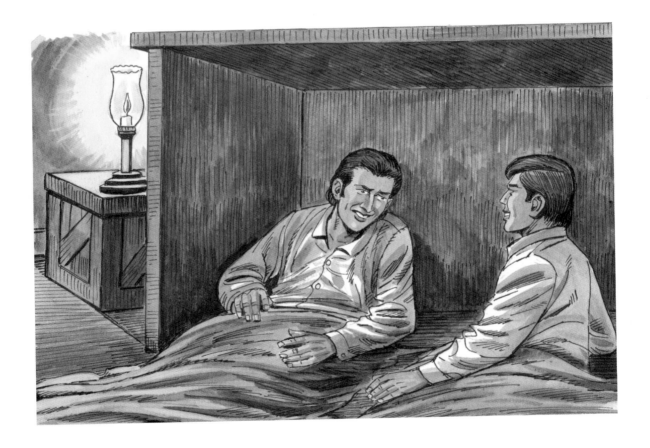

AQA exam-style question

Starting with this extract, explore how Dickens presents the importance of being a good employer in *A Christmas Carol*.

Write about:

- how Dickens presents the importance of being a good employer in this extract

- how Dickens presents the importance of being a good employer in the novella as a whole.

[30 marks]

NAILIT!

When writing about contextual factors, consider:

- what will help me understand the text or the writer's **viewpoint**?

- what might different readers understand about this text?

- what will help to get a better understanding of the themes, language, or characters?

A student has written notes to answer this exam question. They would like to add contextual factors into their essay. Add contextual factors to these notes where appropriate.

Point 1	The Ghost uses language to create a sense of Scrooge's former viewpoints. Scrooge's defence of Fezziwig shows he is 'speaking unconsciously like his former… self'.
Point 2	Dickens presents the qualities of a good employer and an understanding of the power an employer could wield – repetition of 'power'; 'The happiness he gives is quite as great as if it cost a fortune.'
Point 3	How Scrooge is described as an employer elsewhere in the novella, for example, Stave One. Fezziwig is used as a foil to Scrooge as an employer.
Point 4	Theme of redemption; how this memory creates positive change in Scrooge as an employer.
Point 5	Dickens' message about employers shown by how Scrooge behaves at the end of the novella – he values his employees, becoming interested in their lives and welfare.

Belle

Summary

The Ghost declares that time grows short. Scrooge sees himself as an older man in 'the prime of his life'. Belle leaves his former self. She has found he is too obsessed with work and money and leaves little time or love for her – he is not the man she once fell in love with. Belle tells Scrooge that money has replaced her in his affections. She breaks off their engagement, telling him that their 'contract' was made when they were both poor and that he is now a changed man and her love has no value to him. Scrooge begs the Ghost not to show him anymore, but the Ghost forces him to see the next scene. The following scene shows Belle as a happy mother with children. Belle's husband enters the room 'laden with toys and presents'. The family is boisterous and happy. The husband tells Belle that he saw Scrooge that afternoon. Scrooge was alone. Scrooge begs the Ghost to take him away and a struggle takes place. Scrooge seizes the extinguisher cap and presses it on the head of the Ghost, who 'dropped beneath it'. However, Scrooge is unable to hide all of the light and it streams from under it. Scrooge, back in his bedroom, falls into a heavy sleep.

What we learn about Scrooge through Belle

This section reveals Scrooge's downfall into the bitter miser that we saw at the start of the novella. Through Belle, Dickens shows us a different side of Scrooge: Belle once loved Scrooge and he loved her, informing us that he was once considered lovable and able to love, but his love of money came between them. Belle uses religious imagery. The metaphor "golden" idol tells the reader that Scrooge worships money and wealth, not Belle. Scrooge is shown the life that could have been his with a loving family. Dickens contrasts the noise and laughter of Belle's home life with Scrooge's life 'Quite alone'.

Scrooge in decline

Dickens reveals Scrooge's decline by showing the reader the changes to his face. The reader is told [His face] 'had begun to wear the signs of avarice'. Here Dickens uses personification to show the impact of Scrooge's love of money. Through this image, Dickens presents Scrooge as wearing his love of money as someone would wear clothes, visibly and obviously. 'Avarice' is extreme greed for wealth or money, and both the Victorian and contemporary reader understand that this trait is a sin.

DEFINE IT!

idol – an image or a symbol of a god used in worship

DO IT!

Find two more quotations in this section that show Scrooge's decline through the description of his face. Explain how Dickens' presents this decline through the methods he uses.

STRETCH IT!

Charles Dickens, like many Victorian academics, was interested in the 'science' of **phrenology**. Research what this is and find two examples of where this may have influenced Dickens' descriptions of characters in the novella.

Extract 1

The Ghost has shown Scrooge memories of his past life with Belle and scenes of her life surrounded by a loving family, without Scrooge.

Scrooge cannot bear to face the memories of Belle. He has had to face the images of himself alone, like the 'solitary child' he once was. Dickens presents the loving but financially poor family as a contrast to Scrooge's life.

> 'Remove me!' Scrooge exclaimed. 'I cannot bear it!'
> He turned upon the Ghost, and seeing that it looked upon him with a face in which in some strange way there were fragments of all the faces it
> 5 had shown him, wrestled with it.
> 'Leave me! Take me back! Haunt me no longer!'

Notice the images of the faces that pass over the Ghost's face. This Gothic image, so vividly presented, illustrates why there are so many films made of this novella that appeal to a modern audience.

Extract 2

At the end of Stave Two, Scrooge struggles with the Ghost to close down its light and move away from the scenes. Dickens uses light as a positive symbol of emotional warmth, hope and comfort. The Ghost of Christmas Past's light provides understanding of the past memories, showing how we can learn from our past experiences. Notice at the end of the struggle Scrooge is unable to extinguish all of the light, so he is not able to escape from all of his memories.

DO IT!

Read the extract below. Write a paragraph to explain how Dickens presents Scrooge's actions here.

> Scrooge observed that its light was burning high and bright; and dimly connecting that with its influence over him, he seized the extinguisher cap, and by a sudden action pressed it down upon its head.
> The Spirit dropped beneath it, so that the extinguisher covered its whole form; but though
> 5 Scrooge pressed it down with all his force, he could not hide the light, which streamed from under it in an unbroken flood upon the ground.

Character and theme essentials

Christmas

In this stave, we are shown a modern view of Christmas. In the party at Fezziwig's warehouse, we see a Christmas of good cheer; with a feast, dancing and festivity. Dickens is not presenting a religious view of Christmas; instead he shows the power of Christmas to bring people together in joyful celebration. In this stave Dickens shows how the wealthy Fezziwig brings joy to his employees by sharing his wealth and good cheer at Christmas time.

Redemption

In this stave we see Scrooge's journey towards redemption. Dickens shows that shedding light on our memories and learning from them can help us to be better people. Scrooge wishes that he had assisted the carol singer after seeing his 'former self' as a child. He also wishes that he had treated his clerk differently after viewing his memories of Fezziwig as an employer. It is during this stave that the ice begins to crack surrounding his emotional life, enabling his steps towards redemption. It is as though through being able to empathise and feel regret we can move forward. Dickens shows Scrooge experiencing excitement, laughter and sorrow 'with a rapidity of transition'.

Scrooge

During this stave we see Scrooge changing as he takes steps towards his redemption. As the Ghost of Christmas Past shows him scenes from his past, we see how once Scrooge was able to love and was loved by his sister, Fan, and his fiancée, Belle. However, we also see how Scrooge began his decline to become the miser that we met in Stave One. As the Ghost scrolls through the memories that Scrooge has repressed, Scrooge has moments of recognition of past mistakes. We see him begin to feel sorrow and regret. This stave is useful when writing about Scrooge and the theme of greed.

The Ghost of Christmas Past

This strange Spirit shifts between the form of a child and that of an old man. The Ghost radiates the wisdom that we can develop as we age. It is clothed in a tunic showing emblems of summer and winter seasons, symbolising the passing of time. The Ghost's 'gentle touch' has the power to reconnect Scrooge with his memories bringing a consciousness of a 'thousand odours', 'connected with a thousand thoughts, and hopes, and joys, and cares long, long forgotten'.

Think about the three characters that we are introduced to through Scrooge's memories. Complete the table.

Character, what they represent and their function	Key quotation
Fan represents family life and love between family members. Fan is also used by Dickens to provide hints to Scrooge's childhood and the cruelty of by his father. Fan shows that Scrooge had known love as a child, but he had also known neglect and cruelty.	"Father is so much kinder than he used to be"
Fezziwig	
Belle	

REVIEW IT!

1 How long has Scrooge slept since the end of Stave One?

2 How does the Ghost signal its arrival to Scrooge?

3 What does Dickens tell the reader about the Ghost's appearance?

4 What does the light from the Ghost of Christmas Past's head symbolise?

5 Scrooge asks the Ghost why he is there. What is the Ghost's reply?

6 The Ghost indicates a tear on Scrooge's cheek. What does Scrooge reply?

7 When Scrooge sees the 'solitary child' in the schoolroom, how does he react? Why is this important?

8 When Scrooge's sister, Fan, arrives at the school, what news does she give Scrooge?

9 How does Scrooge react when he first sees Fezziwig in the memory?

10 Why does Dickens include this section with Fezziwig?

11 After he watches the party scene, what does Scrooge wish?

12 Belle uses the language of money, telling Scrooge that her love has no importance to him. What does she say?

13 Why does Dickens include this memory of the broken engagement?

14 Why does Dickens show the family scene with Belle, her husband and children?

15 Explain what Scrooge confesses here in this quotation:

> **"**
> I should have liked, I do confess, to have had the lightest licence of a child, and yet to have been man enough to know its value. **"**

16 When Scrooge sees Belle's husband with their daughter, what does he think? What metaphor does Dickens use to show this thought?

17 When Belle's husband sees Scrooge alone in his office, why is he surprised?

18 Who has made the Ghost's extinguisher cap? Explain your ideas.

19 How does Scrooge behave towards the Ghost at the end of the stave?

20 Name three signs from this stave that Scrooge is changing.

Stave Three
The Second of the Three Spirits

The Ghost of Christmas Present

Summary

Scrooge prepares for the visit of the Ghost. (As he gets ready for the Ghost's arrival, Dickens shows a shift in Scrooge's attitude, but also shows that he needs to be open to events that he cannot control.) He hears his name being called from another room. The room has been transformed into a festive scene with holly, ivy and sumptuous Christmas food. (This room is filled with the feast that Scrooge could afford but chooses not to purchase, linking to the invitation to Fred's Christmas dinner – Scrooge was invited but chose not to go.)

The Ghost of Christmas Present is a 'jolly Giant' holding a torch in the shape of Plenty's horn. Scrooge enters timidly and asks for the lessons the Ghost can teach him. (Scrooge is willing to learn from the Ghost – an attitude change.) Holding the Ghost's robe, Scrooge is shown a series of people preparing for Christmas festivities. As they move through these scenes, the Ghost 'sprinkled incense' on the dinners of the most needy and 'a few drops of water' on those who were angry, making their 'good humour' be restored 'directly'. (Poor people would not have had an oven in their home, so dinners were taken to the bakery to roast. Puddings were boiled, so they could be cooked over the fire at home.)

The Second of the Three Spirits

Dickens presents The Ghost of Christmas Present as the essence of Christmas as we understand it within our culture. He can be viewed as a Father Christmas-style character.

DO IT!

Why do you think Dickens portrays the Ghost of Christmas Present as 'very young'. What links can you find between the Ghost's behaviour and youthful behaviour?

References to light, suggesting the knowledge Scrooge will experience. 'To shed light' is to give insight into an idea or situation.

> "…upon this couch there sat a jolly Giant, glorious to see; who bore a glowing torch, in shape not unlike the Plenty's horn, and held it up, high up,
> 5 to shed its light on Scrooge…"

This ghost is 'jolly' – the previous ghost was 'strange'.

The horn of Plenty appears in myths and classical literature, symbolising abundance. Christmas is seen in Western culture as a time for celebration with lavish food and drink.

STRETCH IT!

Scrooge asks the Ghost to teach him and 'let me profit by it'. Why is Dickens' word choice important in this **phrase**?

Extract 1

The Ghost tells Scrooge that people will celebrate Christmas but will still commit bad deeds or sin – part of Dickens' message about Christmas.

> ' There are some upon this earth of yours,' returned the Spirit, 'who lay claim to know us, and who do their deeds of passion, pride, ill will, hatred, envy, bigotry and
> 5 selfishness in our name, who are as strange to us, and all our kith and kin, as if they had never lived. Remember that, and charge their doings on themselves, not us.'

Notice this list of sins is made up of a list of seven sins. The seven deadly sins appeared in Medieval plays, which were based on Christian teaching.

DEFINE IT!

bigotry – prejudice and intolerance

facetious – playful, teasing

kith and kin – family

parapet – low protective wall along the edge of a roof

seven deadly sins – a group of significant sins from Christian teachings: pride, greed, lust, envy, gluttony, wrath and sloth

DOIT!

Look at this description of London:

The Ghost and Scrooge visit a street where people are preparing for Christmas.

> The sky was gloomy, and the shortest streets were choked up with a dingy mist, half thawed, half frozen, whose heavier particles descended in a shower of sooty atoms, as if all the chimneys in Great Britain had, by one consent, caught fire, and were blazing away to their dear hearts' content. There was nothing very cheerful in the climate or the town, and yet was there an air of cheerfulness abroad that
> 5 the clearest summer air and brightest summer sun might have endeavoured to diffuse in vain. For, the people who were shovelling away on the housetops were jovial and full of glee; calling out to one another from the parapets, and now and then exchanging a facetious snowball – better-natured missile far than many a wordy jest – laughing heartily if it went right, and not less heartily if it went wrong. The poulterers' shops were still half open, and the fruiterers' were radiant in their glory

How does Dickens use contrasts in this section? What is Dickens' message here about Christmas?

AQA exam-style question

Starting with this extract, explore how Dickens presents the spirit of Christmas in *A Christmas Carol*.

Write about:

- how Dickens presents the spirit of Christmas in this extract

- how Dickens presents the spirit of Christmas in the novella as a whole.

[30 marks]

NAILIT!

Use the guidance on pages 84–86 to help you plan your answer.

- In your AQA exam, spend up to 15 minutes on understanding the question and planning your answer.

- You will not have the text with you, so make sure that you get used to choosing short quotations or references from memory.

The Cratchits

Summary

The Ghost leads Scrooge to the Cratchits' house. Here Scrooge sees the poor but happy family excitely making dinner – despite its small size. (Here we see the Cratchits' poverty. Mrs Cratchit's gown has been cut and remade to re-use the fabric that has been least worn – but this has happened twice. Peter is wearing his father's old shirt.)

Scrooge asks if Tiny Tim will live. The Ghost foretells that unless things change in the future, Tim will die, before quoting Scrooge's words back to him. (Tiny Tim would have been one of the poor whose death Scrooge referred to in Stave One as decreasing the 'surplus population'. Lack of medical care in the Victorian era meant that, however much the family loved Tiny Tim, they could not help him.) Bob Cratchit toasts Scrooge and Scrooge has the discomfort of seeing Mrs Cratchit's anger at this and the gloom this throws over the family. (The Cratchit family show wealthy Victorian readers that the poor are not criminals but are often hardworking, grateful people. Bob's toast to Scrooge shows him giving thanks for his employment. The reader knows Scrooge to be a hard-hearted employer.)

Scrooge and the Ghost leave the scene and we are shown a series of snapshots of other people celebrating Christmas: families, miners and sailors. While reflecting on the 'lonely darkness', Scrooge hears a 'hearty laugh'.

The Cratchit family

Dickens is presenting his message that despite the Cratchit family's poverty, they are rich in family love and comfort and grateful for all that they have. Dickens felt how the wealthy in society were ignorant of the hardships of the poor. (He will return to this theme later in the stave.) Despite a romantic view of the lower classes, Dickens wanted to show a human side of the poor. Once Scrooge has 'met' Tiny Tim, he is keen to help him. Dickens' criticism of Victorian values is represented by the example of Tiny Tim and his fate.

DO IT!

What does the scene with the Cratchit family in Stave Three tell the reader about the lives of the poor in Victorian times?

STRETCH IT!

Look at the section in Stave Three where we are shown how people spend Christmas (from 'By this time it was getting dark and snowing heavily…' to '…and had known that they delighted to remember him'.)

Write a paragraph to show how Dickens uses the symbol of warmth and brightness and the symbol of music in this section.

Extract 1

Dickens describes the feast at the Cratchits' home on Christmas Day. Having such a feast, particularly a goose, is unheard of for this poor family.

> Notice that we have the return of the narrator here who comments on the scene as dinner is prepared.

> Dickens creates layers within his descriptions of this rare treat of a feast by firstly adding detail using **noun phrases**, and then adding further detail with **alliteration**.

> Use of a vivid verb here paints a picture of adding sugar.

> Dickens also layers details through his use of verbs and then adds alliteration for a more vivid effect.

> "Such a bustle ensued that you might have thought a goose the rarest of all birds; a feathered phenomenon, to which a black swan was a matter of course – and in truth it was something very like it in that house. Mrs Cratchit made the gravy (ready
> 5 beforehand in a little saucepan) hissing hot; Master Peter mashed the potatoes with incredible vigour; Miss Belinda sweetened up the apple-sauce; Martha dusted the hot plates; Bob took Tiny Tim beside him in a tiny corner at the table; the two young Cratchits set chairs for everybody, not forgetting
> 10 themselves, and mounting guard upon their posts, crammed spoons into their mouths, lest they should shriek for goose before their turn came to be helped. At last the dishes were set on, and grace was said. It was succeeded by a breathless pause, as Mrs Cratchit, looking slowly all along the carving-
> 15 knife, prepared to plunge it in the breast; but when she did, and when the long-expected gush of stuffing issued forth, one murmur of delight arose all round the board, and even Tiny Tim, excited by the two young Cratchits, beat on the table with the handle of his knife, and feebly cried 'Hurrah!'"

> Use of a dynamic verb to suggest an energetic and forceful movement, which is further developed with 'long expected gush of stuffing'.

> The adverb 'feebly' describing how Tim speaks, provides a contrast with the life and vigour of the rest of the scene. This reminds the reader that Tiny Tim's health is uncertain.

AQA exam-style question

Starting with this extract, explore how far you agree with the opinion that Dickens presents a sentimental view of the lower classes.

Write about:

- how far Dickens presents the Cratchit family as unrealistic and sentimental in this extract
- how far Dickens presents the Cratchit family as unrealistic and sentimental in the novella as a whole.

[30 marks]

NAILIT!

Use the guidance on pages 84–86 to help you plan your answer.

Ignorance and Want

Summary

Scrooge hears a hearty laugh and he recognises that it is his nephew, Fred. Scrooge is presented with a vision of Fred's Christmas, and his first view is that the family is laughing at Scrooge's response to Fred's invitation. (Once again, Scrooge is confronted by other people's reactions to him. We saw Mrs Cratchit's response earlier and now we see that Fred's guests also react to him with frustration and annoyance. Fred, however, views his uncle with kindness and compassion and says that he is sorry for him.) The party continues with fun and games and Scrooge joins in with the games, playing along and begging the Ghost to let him continue. 'Uncle Scrooge' is used as an answer to one of the games and Fred drinks to his health. Scrooge is so moved by this that he wants to join in with a speech of his own.

The Spirit and Scrooge continue on their travels when suddenly the Ghost grows older. It tells Scrooge that his own life on the Earth is brief and ends at midnight. Scrooge looks at the Ghost's robe and sees a 'claw' 'protruding' from it. Two children – a boy and a girl – are brought out. The Spirit tells Scrooge that they belong to mankind. The boy is Ignorance and the girl is Want. (This image of the two children is straight from a horror film. These two children symbolise the ills of the world – both in the Victorian era and our world today.)

The Ghost warns Scrooge that he should beware of them, but most of all Ignorance as he will bring doom to mankind. Scrooge asks if there is any help for them, but the Ghost quotes Scrooge's words again as he says, "Are there no prisons?... Are there no workhouses?"

As the clock strikes twelve, the Ghost disappears to be replaced by a hooded phantom. (After these images of horror, the Stave ends on a cliffhanger with a further image from Gothic novellas.)

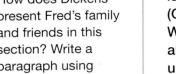

How does Dickens present Fred's family and friends in this section? Write a paragraph using evidence to support your views.

Extract 1

In this extract, Dickens creates drama through his language choices.

> From the foldings of its robe, it brought two children; wretched, abject, frightful, hideous, miserable. They knelt down at its feet, and clung upon the outside of its garment.
>
> 'Oh, Man! Look here! Look, look, down here!' exclaimed the Ghost.
>
> 5 They were a boy and a girl. Yellow, meagre, ragged, scowling, wolfish; but prostrate, too, in their humility. Where graceful youth should have filled their features out, and touched them with its freshest tints, a stale and shrivelled hand, like that of age, had pinched, and twisted them, and pulled them into shreds. Where
>
> 10 angels might have sat enthroned, devils lurked, and glared out menacing. No change, no degradation, no perversion of humanity, in any grade, through all the mysteries of wonderful creation, has monsters half so horrible and dread.
>
> Scrooge started back, appalled. Having them shown to him in this
>
> 15 way, he tried to say they were fine children, but the words choked themselves, rather than be parties to a lie of such enormous magnitude.
>
> 'Spirit, are they yours?' Scrooge could say no more.
>
> 'They are Man's,' said the Spirit, looking down upon them.
>
> 20 'And they cling to me, appealing from their fathers. This boy is Ignorance. This girl is Want. Beware them both, and all of their degree, but most of all beware this boy, for on his brow I see that written which is Doom, unless the writing be erased. Deny it!' cried the Spirit, stretching out its hand towards the city. 'Slander
>
> 25 those who tell it ye. Admit it for your factious purposes, and make it worse. And bide the end.'
>
> 'Have they no refuge or resource?' cried Scrooge.
>
> 'Are there no prisons?' said the Spirit, turning on him for the last time with his own words. 'Are there no workhouses?'

Dickens uses antonyms here which are made more dramatic by the choice of sentence structure.

Dickens uses this short sentence to open the paragraph, creating a dramatic moment.

Repetition emphasises the contrast/opposites in the description of the children: the youth of the children in contrast to their appearance – the wretchedness and comparison with being old (a stale and shrivelled hand, like that of age had warped and distorted them).

Dickens also repeats the use of negative noun phrases 'no…'

The effect of repeated negative noun phrases is to make this negative viewpoint emphatic.

STRETCH IT!

Is this image of 'ignorance' and 'want' still relevant to our society? Can you find any modern parallels?

DO IT!

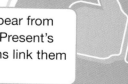

Ignorance and Want appear from the Ghost of Christmas Present's robes. Why does Dickens link them with this Ghost?

Theme and character essentials

Scrooge

In Stave Three we see Scrooge making further steps towards his redemption. He is keen to learn from the Ghost of Christmas Present and is 'not the dogged Scrooge he had been' towards the Ghost, showing that he is now more open towards the Ghost's message. He acknowledges that he has learned from the previous Spirit, and his understanding of 'profit' has moved beyond money to personal improvement. With this Ghost, Scrooge witnesses many people's festive celebrations, but it is the Cratchits' family Christmas that has the most impact on him. Here he sees the warmth of family – even if poor – and this understanding enables him to view his own family festivities. Fred's party shows him what he has been missing each year, and the reader sees Scrooge move on from the pain and anguish from the previous stave as he is excited by the games from Fred's party. Scrooge encounters the children of 'Man', Ignorance and Want, who appal him, and as the Ghost quotes his harsh words back at him, he shows his shame at his previous opinions.

The Ghost of Christmas Present

The Ghost of Christmas Present symbolises the ideal Christmas – the opportunity to celebrate in the warmth of family love and friendship. The Ghost appears on a throne of lavish food representing celebration and generosity. It is important to remember here that this is the feast that Scrooge could afford, yet chose to spend his time alone with a bowl of gruel. For Dickens, Christmas is a time for sharing with family and friends even if there is only a small pudding to share. In the Ghost's visions of the Cratchits, Scrooge is able to witness the love within the family as well as seeing the hardship they face. The Ghost of Christmas Present is presented as compassionate and generous as he supports the poor with his incense, showing how the poor are ignored by the wealthy in society.

Ignorance and Want

These children come straight from a horror film, with their 'wretched' and 'hideous' appearance. Dickens presents these children as being the root cause for all the world's ills. They personify the problems caused in society by wealthy people's indifference towards the poor's 'want', their physical suffering and 'ignorance', their lack of education. Dickens is clear that these children are associated with the Ghost of Christmas Present because they

are part of the problems of his own times. Dickens believed that these issues were key within his society. As they are presented as children, it is suggested that these problems could be solved if society wished it.

However, as these problems still exist today, readers will understand that these messages apply to modern society as well as Victorian society.

DO IT!

Create a chart to help you to quickly identify the visions from each stave as Scrooge makes his journey towards redemption through the novella. Include an explanation of what Scrooge and the reader learn from each vision.

REVIEW IT!

1   What wakes Scrooge up from his deep sleep at the start of Stave Three?

2   How does the Ghost of Christmas Present transform Scrooge's room? Name three things.

3   When Scrooge meets the Ghost of Christmas Present, he behaves differently. Explain how he behaves.

4   Name three foods that are for sale in the street that the Ghost and Scrooge visit.

5   Why are people taking their dinner to the bakery?

6   The Ghost sprinkles incense from his torch on the dinners. What does that do to the dinner?

7   The Ghost sprinkles water onto people. What happens as a result?

8   Name the members of the Cratchit family.

9   Why does Mrs Cratchit worry about the pudding? What doesn't the family worry about?

10 Twice in this stave the Ghost quotes Scrooge's words to him. What does he say?

11 The Spirit shows Scrooge the miners' Christmas celebration. How do they show their Christmas spirit?

12 The Spirit shows Scrooge the lighthouse men's Christmas celebration. How do they show their Christmas spirit?

13 How does Fred feel about Scrooge?

14 How does Scrooge react to the games being played by the guests at Fred's house?

15 Two children emerge from the Ghost's robes. 'The boy is _____. The girl is _____.' Fill the blanks.

16 Dickens uses contrasts to describe these children. Write down one of these contrasts.

17 Who do these children belong to?

18 The Ghost says that we should 'beware them both', but which one should we beware the most?

19 How does Scrooge react to these two children?

20 As the clock strikes twelve, the final Phantom appears. How does Dickens describe it?

Stave Four
The Last of the Three Spirits

The Ghost of Christmas Yet to Come

Summary

The Ghost of Christmas Yet to Come, draped in a black garment, moves towards Scrooge. (This Ghost is terrifying and forbidding and Scrooge fears it.) The only thing left visible of the Ghost is its 'outstretched hand'. It does not speak. Scrooge tells the Ghost that although he is fearful of it, he knows that its purpose is to 'do me good' and for that he is 'thankful'.

Scrooge urges the Phantom to 'Lead on!' and the Ghost takes him to a street where a group of businessmen are discussing the death of someone they all knew. They gossip about his money and how his funeral will be 'cheap'. They don't want to attend the funeral, though one says he will go if lunch is provided. (Dickens presents Scrooge listening to others talking about him again. Here, Scrooge does not realise that the men are talking about his death.)

Scrooge ponders why the Ghost is showing him such a 'trivial' conversation and looks, unsuccessfully for his future self. (Dickens uses **dramatic irony** here. The reader guesses that it is Scrooge who has died, however, we watch Scrooge trying to fit the clues together.)

STRETCHIT!

Research the Grim Reaper. What elements of this cultural figure has Dickens used in his portrayal of the Ghost of Christmas Yet to Come?

Ghost of the Future

DO IT!

"
The Phantom slowly, gravely, silently approached. When it came near him, Scrooge bent down upon his knee; for in the very air through which this Spirit moved
5 it seemed to scatter gloom and mystery. It was shrouded in a deep black garment, which concealed its head, its face, its form, and left nothing of it visible save one outstretched hand. But for this it would have
10 been difficult to detach its figure from the night, and separate it from the darkness by which it was surrounded.
He felt that it was tall and stately when it came beside him, and that its mysterious
15 presence filled him with a solemn dread. He knew no more, for the Spirit neither spoke nor moved.
"

> Dickens uses a list of adverbs to show how the Phantom moves ending with 'silently'.

> This verb suggests that gloom and mystery were flung through the air forcefully.

> Dickens emphasises the dark nature of the Phantom.

1 What does the adverb 'stately' suggest? Why has Dickens chosen it?

2 The Ghost is described as being 'shrouded in a deep black garment'. What does the verb 'shrouded' suggest? Why has Dickens chosen it?

Extract 1

> Dickens shows Scrooge trying to work out why he has been shown these visions. Dickens uses dramatic **irony** to point out that Scrooge should not be 'assured' by these visions. Like Scrooge, the reader recognises that these conversations will be important – but we also realise that it will not be good news for Scrooge.

"
Scrooge was at first inclined to be surprised that the Spirit should attach importance to conversations apparently so trivial; but feeling assured that they must have some hidden purpose, he set himself to consider what it was likely to be. They could scarcely be supposed to have any bearing on the death of Jacob,
5 his old partner, for that was Past, and this Ghost's province was the Future. Nor could he think of any one immediately connected with himself, to whom he could apply them. But nothing doubting that, to whomsoever they applied, they had some latent moral for his own improvement, he resolved to treasure up every word he heard, and everything he saw; and especially to observe the shadow of
10 himself when it appeared. For he had an expectation that the conduct of his future self would give him the clue he missed, and would render the solution of these riddles easy.
He looked about in that very place for his own image, but another man stood in his accustomed corner, and though the clock pointed to his usual time of day for
15 being there, he saw no likeness of himself among the multitudes that poured in through the porch. It gave him little surprise, however; for he had been revolving in his mind a change of life, and thought and hoped he saw his new-born resolutions carried out in this.
"

> The Ghost tells Scrooge that people will celebrate Christmas but will still commit bad deeds or sin – part of Dickens' message about Christmas.

DO IT!

How does Dickens use dramatic irony in this stave? Write a paragraph to explain your thinking.

DEFINE IT!

beetling shop – a shop buying and selling goods that could be reused

charwoman – a cleaner

laundress – a woman who is employed to wash clothes and linen, for example, sheets and towels

undertaker's man – an undertaker prepares bodies for burial or cremation; an undertaker's man works for the undertaker

Sale of goods of a dead man

Summary

The Ghost takes Scrooge to a 'beetling shop' as three characters enter with goods to sell. The undertaker's man shows his goods first: personal items taken from the corpse. (The descriptions of the theft of personal items from a dead man are chilling, even to a modern reader.) The laundress says the man died alone as she brings her goods: some clothes; sheets and towels; silverware and boots. The charwoman brings bed curtains, blankets and the shirt the corpse was wearing to be buried.

The scene changes and Scrooge is standing alongside a bed. With no one to mourn it, a body lies under a sheet. Scrooge is tempted to look under the sheet, but does not; instead he considers the dead man's situation, wondering why the rats are so restless beneath the hearth. The Ghost signals for Scrooge to look at the dead man's head, but Scrooge refuses. (Dickens increases the suspense within the scene as the reader wills Scrooge to look at the face beneath the sheet. Scrooge, unlike the reader, will not guess the identity until later in the stave.)

DO IT!

1 How does Dickens present Joe and the three people who enter his shop?

2 What does Dickens want the reader to learn from this scene?

Writing about language

Here a student is writing about how Dickens presents the dark side of a Victorian city. Look closely at how this student examines the **effect** of Dickens' choice of language.

Dickens layers his description with sensation to build a picture of a corrupted city. He uses pairs of adjectives and nouns linked by 'and' to show that the 'ways' were 'foul and narrow'; the 'shops and houses wretched'. His use of emotive language - 'wretched' - creates a sense of disgust which he further emphasises with a list of overwhelming sensations of 'smell and dirt, and life'. This use of lists overpowers the reader, mirroring how people in the streets would also be overwhelmed by these sensations.

defines the **style** used

identifies Dickens' language choices

identifies the reason for Dickens' choice of style

explains how these choices impact on the reader

explains the impact of those choices

Extract 1

> 'If he wanted to keep 'em after he was dead, a wicked old screw,' pursued the woman, 'why wasn't he natural in his lifetime? If he had been, he'd have had somebody to look
> 5 after him when he was struck with Death, instead of lying gasping out his last there, alone by himself.'

Dickens puts truthful words into the mouth of a character the reader is supposed to dislike and view with suspicion. The suggestion is that if someone so unscrupulous could see this truth, why couldn't Scrooge (or other members of society who may be reading the novella)?

DEFINE IT!

natural – in this context, 'natural' means 'kinder'

plundered – forcibly robbed, as though in a time of war

Extract 2

Notice how Dickens introduces an object or a state of being before adding further information to layer the detail.

> He recoiled in terror, for the scene had changed, and now he almost touched a bed: a bare, uncurtained bed: on which, beneath a ragged sheet, there lay a something covered up, which, though it was dumb, announced itself
> 5 in awful language.
> The room was very dark, too dark to be observed with any accuracy, though Scrooge glanced round it in obedience to a secret impulse, anxious to know what kind of room it was. A pale light, rising in the outer air, fell
> 10 straight upon the bed; and on it, plundered and bereft, unwatched, unwept, uncared for, was the body of this man. Scrooge glanced towards the Phantom. Its steady hand was pointed to the head. The cover was so carelessly adjusted that the slightest raising of it, the motion of a
> 15 finger upon Scrooge's part, would have disclosed the face. He thought of it, felt how easy it would be to do, and longed to do it; but had no more power to withdraw the veil than to dismiss the spectre at his side.

Here Dickens uses the contrast of not speaking/speaking side by side (juxtaposition), creating a feeling of unease.

 STRETCH IT!

In these sections, Dickens shows us the rich and the poor of London. What is his message here?

DO IT!

How do the following characters relate to the theme of greed and to Dickens' message about society:

a the merchants and businessmen?

b the thieves who rob the dead Scrooge?

Emotion at the death

Summary

After seeing the people's reactions to the death, Scrooge begs the Ghost to show him 'any person in the town who feels emotion'. The Ghost takes Scrooge to a room where a woman is waiting for her husband to return. (Throughout the novella, whenever Scrooge overhears a conversation about himself, he never hears anything good. Because of this structural pattern, the reader knows this will not turn out well for Scrooge. This is an example of dramatic irony, which increases suspense.)

A man enters with an expression of 'serious delight' that he is struggling to hide. He tells his wife that it is 'bad' news but they have hope. The man they owe money to is dead. The wife is thankful, though is sorry that this is the first 'emotion' in her heart. The husband says he doesn't know who will take over the debt, but it won't be anyone as 'merciless' as their previous 'creditor'. The house was happier as a result of this death. (Dickens is showing his readers the fate of those who care for money more than human relationships and social responsibility.)

The Phantom

Notice in this stave that the Ghost of Christmas Yet to Come is referred to as a 'Phantom' by Dickens. This term has **connotations** of darkness and death. The Victorian reader would understand its links with the Grim Reaper.

> The Phantom spread its dark robe before him for a moment, like a wing; and withdrawing it, revealed a room by daylight, where a mother and her
> 5   children were.

Dickens uses this simile to suggest the Phantom is like an angel here. However, the reader would see this as a 'dark' or fallen angel.

Notice the contrast between the darkness of the Phantom's robe and the 'daylight' in the room. The scene with the mother and children should present an idyllic, happy scene, but we soon learn that it is filled with anxiety – a further contrast.

DOIT!

The Ghost of Christmas Yet to Come can be linked with death and all that is associated with it. Find three macabre (gruesome and horrible) impressions from this stave that Dickens uses to warn his readers of what could happen to them if they put money and wealth above human relationships.

Extract 1

This is a strong description suggesting that their creditor (the person who lent them money) is cruel, ruthless and without compassion.

> 'To whom will our debt be transferred?'
> 'I don't know. But before that time we shall be ready with the money; and even though we were not, it would be bad fortune indeed to find so
> 5 merciless a creditor in his successor. We may sleep tonight with light hearts, Caroline.'
> Yes. Soften it as they would, their hearts were lighter. The children's faces hushed, and clustered round to hear what they so little
> 10 understood, were brighter; and it was a happier house for this man's death! The only emotion that the Ghost could show him, caused by the event, was one of pleasure.

DEFINE IT!

creditor – a person or a company that you could owe money to; in this case it was Scrooge

A Victorian reader would understand the mixture of feelings the husband and wife would have about this news. In our culture we are taught, even to this day, not 'to speak ill of the dead'. However, the family have a reprieve through this death and cannot help but be 'light'-hearted.

Look at how Dickens delays telling the reader the name of the emotion. He adds clauses, building the suspense until he supplies the name of the emotion, 'pleasure'.

DO IT!

1 Explain why the scene showing the husband and wife's reactions is effective at this point in the novella.

2 Think back over the novella to this point. Find three other instances where Scrooge hears himself being talked about by other characters. Explain briefly why Dickens includes them in the novella.

 STRETCH IT!

Why does Dickens include children in the scene above?

The Death of Tiny Tim

Summary

Distressed, Scrooge asks the Ghost to show him some 'tenderness connected with a death'. The Ghost takes him to Bob Cratchit's house. It is quiet, Mrs Cratchit is sewing and Peter is reading to the children. (Dickens uses the contrast of the noisy family celebration that we saw in Stave Three with the silence of the house and children to show the family's grief.) They are waiting for Bob Cratchit, but he has been walking slowly lately. Scrooge realises that Tiny Tim has died. Bob Cratchit enters and even in his grief he is kind and warm to his family. Bob Cratchit breaks down and goes upstairs to the room where Tim's body lies. (In Victorian times, a body would remain in the home before burial. Often the funeral would also take place in the home. Dickens presents a contrast between the loving treatment of Tim's body and the man completely alone in his room, whose body had also been robbed.) The room is decorated for Christmas. Bob kisses the 'little face' before returning, comforted, to his family.

Bob tells the family of Fred's kindness and they discuss the qualities of Tiny Tim. (Dickens presents a contrast between Fred's behaviour and empathy for the family with what we might expect Scrooge's behaviour to have been in this situation.)

A quiet house

Notice the repetition of 'quiet', the contrast of 'noise' and the lack of movement in this opening paragraph.

DO IT!

Write a paragraph to explain how the Cratchit family is presented in this extract.

> Quiet. Very quiet. The noisy little Cratchits were as still as statues in one corner, and sat looking up at Peter, who had a book before him. The mother and her daughters were engaged in sewing. But surely
> 5 they were very quiet!
> 'And he took a child, and set him in the midst of them.' Where had Scrooge heard those words? He had not dreamed them. The boy must have read them out, as he and the Spirit crossed the threshold. Why did he
> 10 not go on?
> The mother laid her work upon the table, and put her hand up to her face.
> 'The colour hurts my eyes,' she said.
> The colour? Ah, poor Tiny Tim.

The Victorian reader would recognise the Biblical reference, Matthew 18:3. In this text, Christ tells his disciples that to enter the kingdom of heaven they should have faith like a child.

The reader can assume that Mrs Cratchit is sewing funeral clothes in black. This colour is difficult to sew and would hurt her eyes.

Extract 1

A 'green hill' is a symbol of peace and serenity. Here Tim will find rest and peace.

Notice the contrast between Bob's unhappiness and the cheerful lighting in the room Tim slept in. This cheer helps him to compose himself and gives him comfort.

'Sunday! You went to-day, then, Robert?' said his wife. 'Yes, my dear,' returned Bob. 'I wish you could have gone. It would have done you good to see how green a place it is. But you'll see it often. I promised him that
5 I would walk there on a Sunday. My little, little child!' cried Bob. 'My little child!'
He broke down all at once. He couldn't help it. If he could have helped it, he and his child would have been farther apart perhaps than they were.
10 He left the room, and went upstairs into the room above, which was lighted cheerfully, and hung with Christmas. There was a chair set close beside the child, and there were signs of someone having been there lately. Poor Bob sat down in it, and when he had thought a little and
15 composed himself, he kissed the little face. He was reconciled to what had happened, and went down to his family again quite happy.

Notice the repetition of 'little', emphasising Tim's youth. Although child mortality was high at this time, Dickens is showing the reader that this death could have been avoided if the family had not been so poor.

Dickens' description of the room 'hung with Christmas' once again links Christmas with family love and the comfort that brings.

Notice the contrast between this 'kissed' face and the face of the dead man that was covered and abandoned in Stave Three.

Dickens is pointing out to the reader that Tim had a lasting impact on those he came into contact with. He was without wealth but held goodness and wisdom.

DO IT!

Some critics argue that Tiny Tim can be viewed as a Christ figure. How far do you agree with this point of view? You could think about: sacrifice, selflessness and moral purity.

NAIL IT!

In your AQA exam, it is OK to explore your personal response, but do explain your views with reference to details in the text. To show that you are exploring possible **interpretations**, use tentative words.

The Ghost's revelation

Summary

Scrooge senses that the Ghost of Christmas Yet to Come is about to leave him and begs for the Ghost to show him the identity of the dead man. (Scrooge is willing to face the Ghost's visions. Some critics suggest that Scrooge knows that he is the dead man at this point in the novella. You need to decide whether you think Scrooge does suspect.) The Ghost takes him to his former office and points beyond the house. Scrooge looks in the office window but the furniture has changed and he is not the figure in the chair.

They go to a neglected churchyard and the Ghost points to a grave. Scrooge asks him two key questions: are these things set in place or can they be changed? The Ghost continues to point to the name on the stone: Ebenezer Scrooge.

Scrooge realises finally that he is the dead man. He declares he has changed. He pledges to 'honour Christmas in my heart'. (Dickens uses Christmas as a symbol for generosity and the warmth of human relationships. Previously Scrooge shut this out of his heart.) He grabs the Ghost's hand as it collapses and dwindles down into a bedpost.

The climax of the novella

This gesture is as if Scrooge is begging for mercy. This is a contrast to the 'merciless' creditor we heard about earlier in the stave.

This is the climax of the novella – the moment the reader has been eagerly waiting for.

The repetition of 'no' emphasises Scrooge's horror.

> Scrooge crept towards it, trembling as he went; and following the finger, read upon the stone of the neglected grave his own name, EBENEZER SCROOGE.
> 'Am I that man who lay upon the bed?' he cried upon his knees.
> 5 The finger pointed from the grave to him, and back again.
> 'No, Spirit! Oh no, no!'
> The finger still was there.
> 'Spirit!' he cried, tight clutching at its robe, 'hear me! I am not the man I was. I will not be the man I must have been but for this
> 10 intercourse. Why show me this, if I am past all hope?'

Scrooge focuses on 'hope', suggesting that he still wishes for redemption.

DO IT!

What does Scrooge learn in this stave? Write a paragraph to explain your ideas.

STRETCH IT!

Some people argue that the Three Spirits are like the Holy Trinity of the Father, the son and the Holy Spirit in Christian teachings. It certainly seems that Scrooge is able to change and lead a different life after his experiences with the Three Ghosts. How far do you think Dickens is presenting Scrooge's redemption from a Christian point of view?

Extract 1

Scrooge pleads with the Spirit. Look at how Dickens shows Scrooge winning it over.

> For the first time the hand appeared to shake.
> 'Good Spirit,' he pursued, as down upon the ground
> he fell before it: 'your nature intercedes for me, and
> pities me. Assure me that I yet may change these
> 5 shadows you have shown me, by an altered life.'
> The kind hand trembled.
> 'I will honour Christmas in my heart, and try to keep
> it all the year. I will live in the Past, the Present, and
> the Future. The Spirits of all Three shall strive within
> 10 me. I will not shut out the lessons that they teach. Oh,
> tell me I may sponge away the writing on this stone!'
> In his agony, he caught the spectral hand. It sought
> to free itself, but he was strong in his entreaty, and
> detained it. The Spirit, stronger yet, repulsed him.
> 15 Holding up his hands in a last prayer to have his fate
> reversed, he saw an alteration in the Phantom's hood
> and dress. It shrunk, collapsed, and dwindled down
> into a bedpost.

Scrooge continues to pile on the pressure with a threefold pledge to change direction. He emphasises this pledge by the repetition of 'I will' three times, strengthening his commitment to change.

Here we have a striking use of two short sentences about the hand of the spirit and their related **vocabulary** choice ('shake', 'trembled'). Scrooge is pleading with the Spirit, who seems to be changing its mind; the second time the hand is described as 'kind'. The reader understands that Scrooge is getting somewhere.

Interestingly, it is the 'hands in a last prayer' that win the Spirit over, rather than all Scrooge's promises. Again the Spirit's capitulation is emphasised with another threefold repetition, this time repeated verbs that show how the Spirit shrinks: 'shrunk, collapsed, and dwindled.'

DO IT!

1 What is the effect upon Scrooge when he sees his name on the gravestone?

2 Why do you think it takes Scrooge so long to face this truth? You might want to refer to Dickens' message about social responsibility, and the structure of the novella in your response.

AQA exam-style question

Starting with this extract, explore how Dickens presents the idea of transformation in *A Christmas Carol*.

Write about:

• how Dickens presents the idea of transformation in the extract

• how Dickens presents the idea of transformation in the novella as a whole.

[30 marks]

NAIL IT!

Use the guidance on pages 84–86 to help you plan your answer.

To gain the highest marks in your answer in your AQA exam you need to develop a 'conceptual response' to the question. That means starting with a clear and thoughtful point of view.

Character and theme essentials

Christmas

It is interesting that in this stave the features of Christmas festivities recede into the background as Dickens explores the religious nature of moral reckoning where we must prepare to be judged when we die. The only Christmas-like element is the decoration in the room where Tiny Tim's body lies – a sad reminder for the reader that this scene is still set during the Christmas period.

Greed

Perhaps the most distressing portrayal of greed within this stave is the moral corruption of the thieves who strip the dead body of anything worth selling. Dickens shows their callousness as he drives his message home that money is of little use unless it is used to help others. This message is further emphasised by the love shown towards the body of Tiny Tim later in the stave.

Family

We are shown two families in this stave. We see the young family who are waiting for news regarding their debt. This family is presented as 'care–worn' by their poverty, but at the end they are shown 'clustered' together and illuminated by their 'bright' faces. The second family, the Cratchit family, is shown in their grief for their beloved child. Again the family is poor, yet unlike Scrooge's emotional poverty, they are shown in their togetherness as they comfort Bob at the end of the scene. Both of these family scenes show the reader the horror of Scrooge's death 'lying gasping out his last there, alone by himself'.

Scrooge

In this stave, Scrooge witnesses a series of distressing scenes culminating in him seeing his dead body under a sheet, and his gravestone. He is forced to recognise that these scenes are revealing his actual future – they are not merely lessons for him to learn as parallel scenes from someone else's life. The reader observes Scrooge's dramatic transformation as he pledges that he will "honour Christmas in my heart" – a symbol of a life filled with generosity and love for humankind.

The Ghost of Christmas Yet to Come

The Ghost of Christmas Yet to Come represents the future that waits for us all – death. Dickens presents the Ghost as a silent, faceless figure draped in a 'shroud' – a cloth that would wrap a dead body. This shroud represents Scrooge's ominous future where he will be alone, defiled by thieves and unloved by anyone after death.

DO IT!

Write three bullet points to show Dickens' message about social responsibility in this stave.

REVIEW IT!

1 Name three features of the appearance of the Ghost of Christmas Yet to Come.

2 How does Scrooge react to the Ghost?

3 Why do you think Dickens presents the Ghost of Christmas Yet to come as silent?

4 What is the merchants' first reaction to the news about the death?

5 The merchants joke about the funeral. What do they say?

6 What nickname do the businessmen call Scrooge? What does this mean?

7 How did Scrooge feel about the businessmen in his lifetime?

8 How does Dickens show the reader that the businessmen did not care for Scrooge and were not saddened by the death?

9 How does Dickens show the seedy side of poverty in this stave?

10 What were the professions of the three thieves?

11 What could be found in the 'beetling shop'? Name three things.

12 When Mrs Dibner (the third woman) produces her items, why is it shocking for the reader?

13 How does Dickens show that the thieves are not remorseful about stealing from a dead body?

14 When Scrooge is taken to the room with the body, how is the body described as the shaft of light reveals it?

15 How does Dickens show that the man and his wife feel remorse for their 'pleasure' in the death?

16 Where will Tiny Tim be buried?

17 How does Bob Cratchit describe Fred?

18 When Scrooge looks into the window of his office, what is different?

19 Scrooge says that 'I will live in the Past, the Present, and the Future.' What does he mean by this?

20 Explain how the Ghost of Christmas Yet to Come is linked to Fred's comment in Stave One, that all people are 'fellow-passengers to the grave'.

Stave Five
The End of It

'A Merry Christmas to everybody!'

Summary

Scrooge finds himself in his own bed. He knows that he now has time to put right his past behaviour. He gives thanks to Jacob Marley and realises that his face is 'wet with tears'. His joy is clear when he realises that the curtains are still there and he declares himself, 'as light as a feather'. He goes around the fireplace noting elements from his time with the Ghosts, knowing in his heart that 'it's all true, it all happened.' Scrooge laughs and declares himself 'a baby'. (This metaphor illustrates his rebirth and new life.)

Scrooge realises that he doesn't know what day it is and how long he has been with the Spirits. The church bells ring and, looking out of the window, Scrooge sees the fog has lifted and it is a clear day. (Notice that Dickens has used bells here to signal Scrooge's new life. These are 'glorious' bells, unlike those that rang to signal Marley's entrance in Stave One. As a Christian symbol, this signals Scrooge's redemption. Dickens also uses **pathetic fallacy** here to signal that Scrooge's ignorance has lifted and that he is ready for redemption.) He asks a boy what day it is and he is told that it is Christmas day. (Notice how all of the visits from the Ghosts have all happened in one day.)

Scrooge's redemption

Look at how Dickens' use of language shows Scrooge's distress:

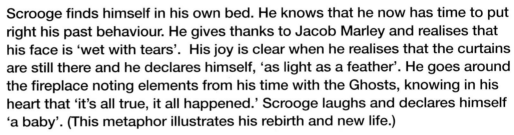

Simple sentence with one straightforward statement. The exclamation mark links to 'cried', indicating the strength of feeling.

Repetition of this clause emphasises his thought process as if he is convincing himself.

> 'They are not torn down,' cried Scrooge, folding one of his bed-curtains in his arms, 'they are not torn down, rings and all. They are here – I am here – the shadows of
> 5   the things that would have been may be dispelled. They will be. I know they will!'

Repeated syntax – the second repetition in parenthesis. Use of 'I' to reassure himself that he is in the present day and that the theft of the curtains was part of the Ghost's visions.

Repeated use of 'will' to assure himself that these terrible visions will not come into being.

DO IT!

At the start of this stave, Dickens tells the reader:

> He was so fluttered and so glowing with his good intentions, that his broken voice would scarcely answer to his call.

How does Dickens show the reader Scrooge's emotional state here?

STRETCH IT!

Research the use of bells in the Christian church. Why has Dickens used this symbol at this point in the novella?

Extract 1

This is a key moment of change for Scrooge.

Notice the repetition of the structure here 'I am….I am…I am…I am…' that emphasises Scrooge's joy.

The change in Scrooge is highlighted by the similes and the adjectives 'light', 'happy', 'merry' and 'giddy' suggesting exuberance and elation.

"

'I am as light as a feather, I am as happy as an angel, I am as merry as a school-boy. I am as giddy as a drunken man. A merry Christmas to everybody! A happy New Year to all the world!
5 Hallo here! Whoop! Hallo!'
He had frisked into the sitting-room, and was now standing there: perfectly winded.

"

Scrooge makes jubilant references to Christmas and good wishes to 'all the world'.

Scrooge's delight overflows into childlike whoops of joy, reinforcing his rebirth and acceptance of that change.

The verb 'frisked', another childlike reference, suggests that Scrooge is dancing and gambolling. The energy used by this has 'winded' him (made him out of breath).

DO IT!

In your AQA exam, you need to explore detailed links between different parts of the novella. Compare the impression of Scrooge we get here at the end of the novella with our impression of him in Stave One when he is coldly in his counting house.

Look at these quotations from this section of Stave Five. Find a quotation from Stave One to show how Scrooge has changed from the start of the novella.

Stave Five	Stave One
'A Happy New Year to all the world! Hallo here! Whoop! Hallo!'	
'I don't know anything. I'm quite a baby. Never mind. I don't care!'	
'…merry bells. Oh, glorious. Glorious!'	

Scrooge and the spirit of Christmas

Summary

Scrooge asks a young boy to buy the 'prize' turkey for delivery to Bob Cratchit's house. Scrooge delights in sending the turkey and his excitement continues as he dresses 'all in his best' and heads out onto the street. (Most families in Victorian times would eat goose as their celebration meal. Turkey was very expensive. The size of this turkey indicates just how much Scrooge has spent on this gift.) Here he smiles and receives Christmas wishes. He sees one of the charity collectors, the 'portly gentleman', and gives him a generous donation before asking the gentleman to visit him rather than give him thanks. (One by one Scrooge puts right his wrongs from the previous day, showing the reader how easy it can be to make changes for the good of society. His behaviour towards the charity worker shows his transformation and contrasts with his behaviour in Stave One.)

Scrooge goes to Fred's house. Summoning his courage, he knocks on the door and goes into the dining room. There he is welcomed with enthusiasm and has a 'won-der-ful' party. The following morning he arrives at the office early, wanting to 'catch Bob Cratchit coming late' into work. Scrooge pretends to be his angry former self but tells Bob that he is going to raise his salary and help his family.

The narrator tells us that Scrooge kept his word and was like 'a second father' to Tiny Tim, who did not die. Scrooge is known for knowing 'how to keep Christmas well' and the story ends with words from Tiny Tim: "God bless us, every one!" (Dickens ends with Tiny Tim's words, both referring to the Christian values of the novella and the goodness within Tiny Tim. It is a hopeful and uplifting ending.)

DO IT!

In your AQA exam, you will need to explore detailed links between different parts of the novella. In Stave Five, Scrooge makes amends for his actions in Stave One. Give five examples of these actions and find quotations from Stave One and Stave Five to illustrate this change. The first column been completed to help you.

Focus	Stave One	Stave Five
Bob Cratchit's working conditions		
Bob Cratchit's pay		
Fred's invitation		
The charity collection		
Tiny Tim		

Extract 1

Here the voice of the narrator closes the story. If this were a shot from a film, we would be 'zooming out'.

This clause reassures the reader, almost as an aside, that Tiny Tim lived.

> Scrooge was better than his word. He did it all, and infinitely more; and to Tiny Tim, who did *not* die, he was a second father. He became as good a friend, as good a master, and as good a man, as the good old City knew,
> 5 or any other good old city, town, or borough, in the good old world. Some people laughed to see the alteration in him, but he let them laugh, and little heeded them; for he was wise enough to know that nothing ever happened on this globe, for good, at which some people did not
> 10 have their fill of laughter in the outset; and knowing that such as these would be blind anyway, he thought it quite as well that they should wrinkle up their eyes in grins as have the malady in less attractive forms. His own heart laughed: and that was quite enough for him.

If we needed any convincing that Scrooge was a reformed character, this seven-fold repetition of 'good', tolling like a Christmas bell, would help to convince us.

Dickens links descriptions of facial movements when laughing with clear sounds of laughter, to emphasise Scrooge's joy. This description of laughter moves from mocking laughter to a 'heart' filled with the laughter of sheer happiness.

Look at this extract from a student's reaction to Scrooge's redemption at the end of the novella:

So after all of his meanness and coldness, it seems to me that Scrooge managed to escape from spending an eternity roaming the earth in torment by going to Fred's party and buying a turkey. What about all of the other things he did, and the sins he committed other than the ones over various Christmases? I think Dickens lets Scrooge off too lightly.

How far do you agree with this point of view? Explain your answer.

NAILIT!

It is important to know the openings and endings of your set texts well. Make sure that you revise these sections of the text before your examination.

Character and theme essentials

Redemption

A Christmas Carol culminates with Scrooge putting right his past mistakes. He provides food for the Cratchit family with the anonymous gift of the prize turkey. He is thoughtful towards the boy he sends on the errand by paying him handsomely, which is a direct contrast to his treatment of the young carol singer who he frightens away in Stave One. Scrooge gives the charity collector a generous donation and opens his heart to family warmth as he joins Fred and his friends and family for their Christmas party. Notice that all of the people he meets treat him with warmth and acceptance. Dickens is showing us that if we seek redemption, we will be forgiven for past mistakes: this is a Christian message reflecting the **context** of the time.

Social responsibility

Scrooge's new-found sense of social responsibility is illustrated through his generosity towards the young boy who helps him to purchase the turkey for the Cratchit family and his donation to the charity collectors. This generosity enables him to open his heart to the warmth of friendship as he asks the charity collector to 'see' him.

Family

Scrooge's welcome by Fred into his family gathering illustrates the generosity of the Christmas spirit that Fred embodies. Scrooge is nervous and hesitant before he enters but we are told that he 'was at home in five minutes'. Through Fred's compassion and generosity, Dickens shows us that forgiveness will be given if we try to redeem ourselves. Scrooge is also welcomed into the Cratchit family. Bob Cratchit, who is the embodiment of a good and loving father-figure, is joined in that role by Scrooge who becomes 'a second father' to Tiny Tim.

DO IT!

Write a paragraph to show how Dickens presents the themes of greed and poverty in this stave.

Scrooge

Stave Five begins with Scrooge's relief and excitement as he wakes in his bed on Christmas morning. This is his rebirth. He is 'quite a baby' and is as 'merry as a school-boy'. Scrooge has the opportunity to put right all of his past mistakes, and through a rapid series of encounters, the reader is shown Scrooge doing just that.

REVIEW IT!

1   In the opening of Stave Five, Scrooge is delighted that the bedpost is 'his own'. Why is this?

2   Why does Scrooge give thanks to Jacob Marley at this point in the novella?

3   Scrooge describes himself as 'quite a baby'. What is this metaphor important?

4   Dickens describes the bells ringing. How are these bells different to the bells in Stave One?

5   Dickens uses pathetic fallacy to describe the weather in this stave. Why does he use this device here?

6   Scrooge buys a turkey for Bob Cratchit. Why is it important that it is a turkey?

7   Dickens describes the size of the turkey. How big is it? Why is this significant?

8   Why is the door-knocker important? What is the effect of returning to it now?

9   Dickens emphasises that Scrooge 'chuckled' as he shaved and dressed. Why is this important? What is the effect of this?

10 Besides chuckling, what else was Scrooge doing to interrupt his shaving? Why does Dickens add this detail?

11 When Scrooge goes into the street and greets people with a 'delighted smile', how do they react?

12 When Scrooge meets the charity collector, he gives a generous donation, but also asks for something in return. What is that? Why is it important?

13 What is Fred's reaction to Scrooge's request to join the family for dinner?

14 What is Bob Cratchit's excuse for being late to work?

15 How does Scrooge react to Bob's excuse for being late? What does this show the reader about Scrooge's redemption?

16 Dickens uses a warm fire to symbolise the warmth of human friendship at the end of this stave. How does he do this?

17 What happened to Tiny Tim at the end of the novella?

18 Who takes over the story at the end of the novella? Why does Dickens do this?

19 Scrooge gives his word to Bob Cratchit that he will 'raise your salary and endeavour to assist your struggling family'. What quotation tells the reader that he keeps his word?

20 Who has the last words in the novella? What are they? Why is this significant?

Characters

Ebenezer Scrooge

What we know about Scrooge

- He is a cold and heartless miser at the start of the novella.

- He has a nephew, Fred, who is son of his now deceased sister, Fan.

- His dead partner in business, Jacob Marley, visits him to issue a warning to change his ways and to tell him that he will be visited by Three Spirits.

- He is visited by the Ghost of Christmas Past, who shows him visions of his past life, including his unhappy childhood, his past employer and his broken engagement to Belle.

- He is visited by the Ghost of Christmas Present, who shows him visions of how others spend Christmas, including the Cratchits and Fred.

- He is visited by the Ghost of Christmas Yet to Come, who shows him visions of Christmas in the future. These visions include the body of a man who died alone and uncared for. Scrooge finally discovers that the visions are showing him his own future.

- He redeems himself by taking the spirit of Christmas into his heart and helping those around him.

Scrooge the miser

Scrooge is initially presented as a cold-hearted miser, who hates Christmas and is 'as solitary as an oyster'. He is 'hard and sharp as flint', suggesting his inflexible and brittle nature. He carries a 'frosty rime' on his head – a metaphor that presents him as cold and frozen to the warmth of human connections. Here are two students writing about their impressions of Scrooge in Stave One:

Student answer A

Our first impression of Scrooge in Stave One is that he is an unfeeling employer with a 'tight-fisted hand at the grindstone' suggesting that he works his employees hard, yet as he is 'tight-fisted' he doesn't share his money through generous wages showing 'the cold within him' extends to his business life as well as his personal life.

Student answer B

In Stave One, the modern reader understands why Scrooge spends his days keeping 'his eye upon his clerk' making sure that the clerk is working hard. Scrooge was not born wealthy as we saw in Stave Two, so the modern reader understands his approach as an employer.

Scrooge as 'the solitary child'

Does Dickens want us to see Scrooge as naturally cold and miserly or as a person who becomes cold and miserly through circumstances and the choices he has made in his life? Through the visions shown by the Ghost of Christmas Past, Dickens presents Scrooge as being capable of love for his sister Fan and capable of inspiring love from Belle. The ice in Scrooge's cold heart seems to have begun when love of money became his 'golden idol' rather than Belle. However, the 'solitary child' that Dickens shows us in Stave Two has become the man who is 'solitary as an oyster' in Stave One. It is interesting that Dickens repeats this emotive word 'solitary'. When it is linked with the noun 'child', we are encouraged to sympathise with Scrooge. When it is linked to 'oyster' in the simile, we see him as closed off from the world, shut off by his hard shell of greed.

Scrooge's redemption

In the final stave, Dickens shows the reader the possibility of change and its role in bringing joy to the world as his theme of redemption is presented through Scrooge's journey. Here we see him in Stave Five 'as light as a feather' and 'as merry as a schoolboy', directly contrasting with 'hard and sharp as flint' in Stave One. This metaphor with the weight of the 'flint' juxtaposing the weightless 'feather' shows the reader Scrooge's happiness. This links with Dickens' message – that the wealthy should help the poor to benefit society.

How do *we* feel about Scrooge?

Surely Scrooge and his attitude towards the poor in Stave One will appal a modern reader, yet these were commonly held views in the Victorian era. Of course, how we feel about Scrooge depends on who 'we' are. Perhaps a Victorian reader might not feel the same sympathy towards him as he changes and develops through the novella as a modern reader might. However, Dickens was viewed in his time as a social reformer and more than 6000 copies of *A Christmas Carol* were sold on publication.

NAILIT!

In your AQA exam, it is worth considering how attitudes of modern and Victorian readers might differ.

Look at this list of words that *might* be appropriate to Scrooge:

unwise   miserable   comical   shrewd   rude   brave   self-pitying   lonely   evil

1   Think carefully about these nine words and put them into a rank order from the most to the least true. You might find that the top half of your rank order contains both negative and positive words.

2   Find evidence to support your top three word choices.

The Ghosts

What we know about the function of the Ghosts

Dickens uses the Ghosts as a device to explore his social message focusing on: the impact of poverty and society's responsibility in easing poverty and how we can all move towards redemption.

- **Jacob Marley** starts the narrative by issuing his warning to Scrooge. He also sets the structure of the novella by introducing the visitation of Three Spirits. Jacob Marley signals Dickens' message of social responsibility when he corrects Scrooge for complimenting him as being a 'good man of business': 'Mankind was my business. The common welfare was my business; charity, mercy, forbearance, and benevolence, were, all, my business.'

- **The Ghost of Christmas Past** shows the actions and the events that have formed Scrooge's past life and how the choices he made during his past have made him the man he is in the present.

- **The Ghost of Christmas Present** shows, through the symbol of Christmas festivities, the warmth of family love from which Scrooge has cut himself off. However, this Ghost also has Ignorance and Want within its robes, signalling a warning about these ills within society.

- **The Ghost of Christmas Yet to Come** shows what will lie in Scrooge's future if he continues on this current path. Unless he redeems himself he will die alone and uncared for. He will also certainly face a tormented eternity 'fettered' in chains like Jacob Marley.

DEFINE IT!

fettered – tied up with chains, especially around the ankles

How should we feel about the Ghosts?

We are probably more fascinated by the Ghosts in *A Christmas Carol* than terrified. Dickens presents them as distinct characters rather than the evil and menacing spectres that can be found in Gothic **fiction**. Even the most terrifying Ghost of Christmas Yet to Come has a 'kind hand' before departure, rather than the hand that was pointing towards the gravestone earlier in the stave. Modern readers, used to horror films, will not view the Ghosts as frightening. Like the Victorian reader, they will see them as symbols of Scrooge's redemption.

STRETCH**IT!**

What other words could be used to sum up Jacob Marley? Choose two words *not* on the list on the left and explain why they are particularly true of Marley.

DO**IT!**

Here are some words, which *might* be used about the different ghosts in the novella:

gentle quiet unhappy silent commanding desperate evil jolly shifting warning welcoming excited joyful unrelenting imposing guiding

1 Choose the two words from the list above that you think are *most* true of each of the three Christmas Spirits.

2 Explain your choices with reference to language and events in the text.

3 Does your choice differ at different points in each stave?

Writing about Dickens' presentation of the Ghosts

Read part of what one student wrote about Jacob Marley. Notice how they use evidence to support their points:

> I don't know how I feel about Jacob Marley. I know that he returns to help Scrooge to start on his journey towards redemption, but I also know that the reason he is 'fettered' with 'the chain I forged in life' is because when he did have the opportunity to help others he kept his 'eyes turned down'. However, we know that he appears before Scrooge that evening to 'warn' him that he has a chance to escape his 'fate' 'with a chance and hope of my procuring' that he has somehow engineered. (Dickens does not explain how.) Scrooge declares that 'You were always a good friend to me', but later in the novella we are told by Belle's husband that Scrooge was alone in his counting house as Jacob Marley was on his deathbed. Seemingly, Scrooge's idea of friendship doesn't extend to being there at times of need. It is only in Stave Five that Scrooge is ready to understand friendship in his care for Tiny Tim.

NAIL**IT!**

In your AQA exam, when you write about a character, make sure you make clear points in answer to the question and back up your points by referring to events and language in the novella.

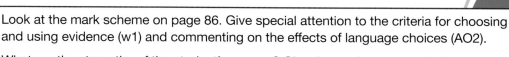

DO**IT!**

Look at the mark scheme on page 86. Give special attention to the criteria for choosing and using evidence (w1) and commenting on the effects of language choices (AO2).

What are the strengths of the student's answer? Give the student some brief advice about how to improve their answer.

A typical AQA exam-style question about ghosts and the supernatural might be:

AQA exam-style questions:

- *[Starting with this extract,]* explore how Dickens presents the supernatural in *A Christmas Carol*.

- *[Starting with this extract,]* explore how Dickens presents the Ghosts as messengers for social change in *A Christmas Carol*.

Other characters

Bob Cratchit

Bob Cratchit represents the deserving poor – a section of society that was viewed by the wealthy classes as deprived, but hardworking and honest. In Stave One he is seen as timid in the face of Scrooge's coldness, but Fred's Christmas spirit gives him cheer. He 'involuntarily' applauds Fred's passionate speech about Christmas, linking him to Fred and what he represents. Later in the novella, he reports Fred's respectful condolences after Tiny Tim is revealed to have died, showing how kindness and consideration from more wealthy people can impact on the poor.

Bob Cratchit, as a father, represents the influence that family can have on adult development. Bob is presented as a loving father in contrast to the picture we are given of Scrooge's father. Fan reports that 'Father is so much kinder than he used to be', leaving the reader to fill the gap of what cruelties added to the 'hard as flint' Scrooge. Scrooge becomes a 'second father' to Tiny Tim at the end of the novella, assuming the role of protector of disadvantaged and needy members of society.

Tiny Tim

Despite his weakness, Tiny Tim is a character representing 'goodness', and his death in the vision leads to Scrooge's redemption. Through this event Dickens is linking Tim to the Christian message of Christ dying to save mankind from sin. Dickens gives him the final words of the novella, words that show his love of humanity as he calls, 'God bless us, every one!' A further link to the Christ-figure is shown as Dickens explains, 'He hoped the people saw him in the church, because he was a cripple, and it might be pleasant to them to remember upon Christmas Day, who made lame beggars walk, and blind men see.' Tim is presented as selfless in the face of his disadvantages, a direct contrast to the wealthy, but selfish, Scrooge.

Fred

Fred represents the spirit of Christmas, the opposite of Scrooge and his values. Fred consistently invites Scrooge to his home despite Scrooge's refusals and shows that he feels sorry for his uncle. He tells guests that Scrooge's 'offences carry their own punishment'. Fred's arrival in the counting house shows him as heat to Scrooge's 'cold'. Fred is hope for the future of the Scrooge family.

NAILIT!

In your AQA exam, think about how different ways characters have been used by Dickens to present his social message. Use words such as 'perhaps', 'might', 'could be' to help you consider more than one view of a character or theme.

Belle

Belle's function is to show that Scrooge was capable of love but his decline through his focus on money and wealth means that he loses love. Her happiness with her family is more than Scrooge can 'bear' as he demands to be removed from the visions. Belle is associated with the theme of greed as Scrooge loses her love through his hunger for money.

DO IT!

What do you think are the five most important things to remember about the Cratchit family? Use the bullet points below.

- Find five quotations.
- Summarise the Cratchit family's symbolic significance.
- Link the Cratchit family to messages about wealth and class.

REVIEW IT!

1   Who is remembered for 'how patient and how mild he was'?

2   What does 'miserliness' mean?

3   Who is being described here? 'No warmth could warm, no wintry weather chill him.'

4   When Bob Cratchit enters the counting house with a coal shovel, what does Scrooge threaten him with?

5   What does this threat show the reader about Scrooge?

6   What does Scrooge tell Fred should happen to people to say 'Merry Christmas' to one another?

7   When Scrooge sees the Ghost of Jacob Marley, he doesn't believe it to be there. What does he put it down to?

8   What does this reaction to the Ghost tell the reader about Scrooge?

9   Bob Cratchit proposes a toast to Scrooge in Stave Three: 'I'll give you Mr. Scrooge, the Founder of the Feast!' What does this show about his character?

10   How does the Cratchit family react to this toast? Why is this important? Explain your ideas in a paragraph.

11   What does this quotation show the reader about Fred?

> 'I'll keep my Christmas humour to the last. So A Merry Christmas, uncle!'

12   In three words describe the Ghost of Christmas Past.

13   In three words describe the Ghost of Christmas Present

14   In three words describe the Ghost of Christmas Yet to Come.

15   Whose seat by the fire is described as 'vacant' by the Ghost of Christmas Present?

16   Who or what does Belle tell Scrooge has replaced her in his heart?

17   What is Scrooge shown at the climax of the novella?

18   Who is described as 'without an angry word'?

19   Who has the last line of the novella? What is that line?

20   Explain which character – other than Scrooge or the Ghosts – could be seen as the most important character in the novella.

Themes and contexts

Social responsibility

In Victorian England there were great contrasts between the wealthy and the poor. Rich people were able to gain from the Industrial Revolution, while people were starving and being ignored by those able to help them. In 1834 the Poor Law Amendment Act was passed. This act introduced a system of workhouses designed to take the place of poor relief (help for the poor) through private charities or public donations. Dickens was critical of this system and ridicules it in many of his novellas, including *A Christmas Carol*. We see Scrooge asking the charity collectors, 'Are there no work houses?' He goes on to voice the viewpoint of many wealthy Victorians, that the poor were lazy and this was the reason for their poverty. Through his portrayal of the Cratchit family, Dickens is able to show that these hardworking and genuinely good people could be caught in the poverty trap. Marley tells Scrooge, 'The common welfare was my business', as he warns Scrooge that he must help before it is too late. The Ghost of Christmas Present's 'Ignorance and Want' act as a warning to society of what will happen if we do not accept our responsibilities towards the poor. A typical AQA exam-style question about social responsibility might be:

STRETCHIT!

Research the Victorian economist Malthus. What did he say about poverty and how does Dickens use his views in *A Christmas Carol*?

AQA exam-style question:

- *[Starting with this extract,]* explore how Dickens presents social responsibility in *A Christmas Carol*.

Christmas

As people began their Christmas preparations, Dickens saw the suspicions wealthy people felt towards the poor fading. Whatever people's wealth or status, they would celebrate. In *A Christmas Carol* we are shown the charity collectors gathering donations for the poor, family parties and workplace parties. Dickens describes Christmas in a series of locations, all showing the warmth and generosity of the season with time spent with loved ones.

Dickens sets these events within the Christmas period because they represent a time when we should be generous towards others. His positive depiction of Christmas is embodied by Fred, the Cratchit family and Fezziwig. Scrooge's 'Humbug!' reaction to the festival is presented as needing to change. At the end, Scrooge can look fondly at Christmas because he was able to make amends and achieve redemption, Scrooge is saved by Christmas.

The novella's title also refers to the Christmas festival with a 'Carol' being a hymn sung at Christmas time. The chapters of the novella are referred to as 'staves' and like the musical notation, there are five horizontal lines in a stave as there are five staves in the novella.

Redemption

Redemption being freed from sin, error or evil. In the novella this redemption is linked with Christian principles. Through the structure of the narrative, Dickens presents Scrooge's journey towards his redemption. At the start of the novella he is presented as a miserly, cold character who is seen rudely rejecting all opportunities for family warmth and love, instead choosing to remain alone and shut off from the generosity that can be found at Christmas. Scrooge is subjected to a series of trials where he is shown the impact of his thinking and behaviour by the Ghosts. He escapes an eternity of torment by embracing the spirit of Christmas and its values by transforming his beliefs to accept responsibility for those in society who need his help. Dickens shows his reader that if Scrooge can change, then anyone can.

Writing about redemption in *A Christmas Carol*

See how one student tries to establish a clear and original point about the role of redemption in *A Christmas Carol*. An examiner has made some notes alongside.

In Stave One, Scrooge is presented as a misanthropic character in need of redemption because he only cares about himself and his wealth. He embodies the ideals and beliefs of many wealthy people that Dickens protests against; stating that 'those who would rather die' than go to the workhouse should do it to 'decrease the surplus population'. Jacob Marley warns Scrooge of the 'incessant torture of remorse' unless he achieves redemption. Marley, himself 'fettered' in chains, tells Scrooge that the chain of his making is 'was full as heavy and as long as this, seven years ago. Yet, ironically, Jacob Marley is unable to achieve redemption for himself despite this act of selflessness. He must, like the phantoms outside the window, witness human need without having the 'power' to 'interfere' in human matters.

Clear and plausible point of view.

Examples strengthen the opening statement.

Practical effects of not caring about others in society are identified to develop the idea.

Interesting angle: Scrooge has been given a unique opportunity to make changes to achieve redemption.

DO IT!

Find examples of Scrooge's steps towards redemption in the novella. Here are two to get you started:

Scrooge weeps when he sees his boyhood home in Stave Two, showing a glimpse of emotion for the first time: 'Your lip is trembling… and what is that upon your cheek?'

Scrooge regrets not giving something to the boy singing a Christmas carol at his door: 'I should like to have given him something: that's all!' (Stave Two)

Greed

A novella that shows the need for a miser to redeem himself is bound to examine greed and the effect of greed on individuals and on society. The scene between Belle and Scrooge in Stave Two where she breaks off their engagement sums up the impact of this greed on human relationships. She says that she has been 'displaced' by 'a golden idol' in his affections and questions whether he would still make their 'contract' as a wealthy man. She uses the language of money, telling him that everything that gave their love 'worth or value' has changed.

DO IT!

Find at least two other examples of the language of greed and/or money in *A Christmas Carol*.

Explain the *effects* of these examples.

Poverty

On the surface, *A Christmas Carol* is a jolly Christmas story with some boisterous family parties and some ghosts. However, Dickens' tale has a clear message for his readers regarding the impact of poverty on society. This is shown most graphically through 'Ignorance' and 'Want', the two hellish children who appear from the robes of the Ghost of Christmas Present. They symbolise the needs of the poor and the ignorance of the wealthy classes of those needs. In their facial features, the signs of poverty are clear, described as 'pinched' and 'twisted' as they 'glared out menacing'. Ignorance is the most dangerous because, as Dickens explains, he has 'Doom' written on his brow unless it is erased.

Dickens' message regarding the workhouses is clear in the novella. Scrooge's words are quoted back to him when he asks if there is any 'refuge or resource' available to help the two children as the Ghost asks, 'Are there no prisons?' With the Poor Law Amendment Act, parishes were not allowed to hand out food, clothing or blankets to those in need. Instead they had to enter a workhouse. There they were treated as if they had caused their poverty themselves – even if they were young, old or ill – and they were treated as though they should be punished. A typical AQA exam-style question about poverty or the poor might be:

DO IT!

Find three further examples of poverty in *A Christmas Carol*.

AQA exam-style questions:

- *[Starting with this extract,]* explore how Dickens presents the impact of poverty on society in *A Christmas Carol*.
- *[Starting with this extract,]* explore how Dickens presents the poor working classes in *A Christmas Carol*.

Family

When Fred enters the counting house, the reader realises Scrooge is not alone because he has no family, instead it is a choice that he has made in his life. Fred brings the family warmth into the counting house. This warmth is seen again in the noise and colour of the Cratchit family. As Dickens' symbols of goodness, their love shows Scrooge the life he lost when he lost Belle's love. A typical AQA exam-style question about family might be:

AQA exam-style question:

[Starting with this extract,] explore how Dickens presents family relationships in *A Christmas Carol*.

Write about:

- how Dickens presents family relationships in this extract
- how Dickens presents family relationships in the novella as a whole.

Read this paragraph from one student's answer to the question above:

One important aspect of family relationships is the human warmth they bring into people's lives. This warmth is shown in opposition to the cold that surrounds Srooge. Fezziwig, Scrooge's former employer, acts as family as he refers to his apprentices as 'my boys!' before he bids them to 'Clear away!' for the party where 'fuel was heaped on the fire.' The warmth and generosity of this party contrasts with Scrooge's 'frosty rime' in his workplace. When Fred, Scrooge's nephew, enters this workplace, the counting house, he brings with him the warmth of family relationships and a 'glow' about his person. This glow symbolises his goodness and is reinforced by further light images surrounding it. Fred's face is 'ruddy' implying he is red and healthy-looking and his eyes 'sparkled', referencing light. Dickens shows how Scrooge rejects the warmth of family relationships represented by Fred, in the same way that he closed himself off from Belle's romantic love to pursue money and wealth.

Notice how this student uses evidence. First, they make a clear point that is directly relevant to the exam question and then back up their point with textual references. Here those references are neatly built into the student's own sentences.

The student refers to words from the question to keep their response on track.

Useful exploration of the connotations of one word and their symbolism.

The paragraph ends with an original insight into what Dickens might be implying about Scrooge and love in all of its forms.

NAIL IT!

When revising themes, build up a useful list of words linked to that theme.

DO IT!

Write down at least five words that are relevant to the theme of redemption in this extract and the novella as a whole.

Next to each word write its definition.

Here is one word to start you off: 'improvement'.

Motifs and symbols

Music

Music winds its way through the novella like a chorus from a Christmas song that gives the novella its name. It is a symbol of happiness and the warmth of shared, community events. We are shown lighthouse men in harsh conditions where one 'struck up a sturdy song that was like a gale itself', and a cheerful company around a 'glowing fire' singing the chorus of 'a Christmas song'. The characters who are seen as 'good' characters within the novella are all linked to music and laughter: Fezziwig's dancing to the fiddler at the party; the noise of Tiny Tim's 'active little crutch on the floor' and beating 'the table with the handle of his knife'. However, it is Fred's 'musical family' who shows Scrooge the value of music in his life. Here Dickens tells us that if Scrooge could have listened to the music his niece is playing 'often, years ago, he might have cultivated the kindnesses of life for his own happiness with his own hands'.

Weather

Weather is used as a **motif** to explore Scrooge's emotions and the state of his soul. Fog represents Scrooge's ignorance about the poor within society and his emotional isolation. This fog comes 'pouring in at every chink and keyhole'. It is inescapable in its density and it obscures all clear sight of society as it makes 'the houses opposite… mere phantoms'. At the end of the novella, when Scrooge has pledged that he will redeem himself, this fog has lifted. As he looks out of the window on Christmas morning there is, 'No fog, no mist; clear, bright, jovial, stirring, cold;' Dickens links this to the motif of music as this bright day is 'piping for the blood to dance to'.

DO IT!

Find examples of the motif of cold/heat and write a paragraph to explain how Dickens uses this motif in the novella.

Marley's chains

Marley's chains symbolise his focus on money and making money rather than helping the people around him. Marley 'wears the chain I forged in life'. The verb 'forged' suggests that these chains were created and shaped with industry. The chains are made 'of cash-boxes, keys, padlocks, ledgers, deeds, and heavy purses wrought in steel'. All of these items are linked to business and making money. They bind him, were made by his 'own free will' and now he has 'No rest. No Peace. Incessant torture of remorse.' Dickens warns the reader that the things you focus on in life will bind you after you die. Marley tells Scrooge that his chain 'was full as heavy and as long as this, seven Christmas Eves ago'. Dickens' depiction of Marley's fate links to the Roman Catholic Christian concept of Purgatory. Purgatory is where sins are purged after death.

Scrooge's bed

The Ghost of Christmas Past enters by drawing 'aside' the bed curtains with its 'hand'. The Ghost of Christmas Yet to Come is shown to have 'shrunk, collapsed, and dwindled down into a bedpost'. A bed is a private space that can also be seen to represent a sanctuary. In Stave Four, Dickens shows how the thief who steals the bed curtains desecrates this space. She is able to do this because the body is unloved and uncared for.

Scrooge's gravestone

The gravestone shown to Scrooge by the Ghost of Christmas Yet to Come, neglected and untended, represents his isolation from any loving human relationships. There is no one to care for the gravestone in a similar way to there not being anyone to care for the body lying in the room.

Bob Cratchit's pay rise

The pay rise that Scrooge gives Bob Cratchit at the end of Stave Five is symbolic of how wealthy employers can help to support their employees. The reader has seen that Bob Cratchit is a good-hearted and loyal employee when he toasts Scrooge despite his family's more realistic view of Scrooge (seen through Mrs Cratchit's outspoken view of Scrooge as 'such an odious, stingy, hard, unfeeling man as Mr Scrooge'). Fezziwig is also symbolic of a good employer who 'has the power to render us happy or unhappy' and chooses happiness, unlike Scrooge at the start of the novella.

DO IT!

What do each of the Ghosts symbolise? Look back through this *AQA GCSE 9–1 English Literature Study Guide* to help you.

NAILIT!

- For the purposes of your AQA exam, a context is only relevant if it sheds light on the novella and your exam question.

- Answering your exam question carefully and thoughtfully is the best way to help you consider the novella's context.

- Do not write down contextual information *for its own sake*.

Contexts

Writing about contexts

Context means one or all of the following:

- ideas and influences at the time the novella was written

- ideas and expectations a modern audience or reader might bring to the novella

- how an extract fits into the whole novella.

Using information about contexts

Here are parts of two different students' responses to a question about how Dickens presents poverty. The references to context are underlined.

Student answer A

When Scrooge responds to the charity collectors with the question designed to shock, 'Are there no prisons?', the reader sees that <u>Dickens is satirically presenting the viewpoints of some members of the contemporary wealthy classes.</u> <u>The widely held opinion that poverty came from a lack of willingness to work</u> is shown as Scrooge refers to the poor as 'idle people', telling the charity collectors that he helps to 'support' prisons and the 'union workhouses'. <u>A Victorian reader as well as a modern reader would recognise this opinion</u> within the more privileged members of society. <u>They, like Scrooge, did not understand the difficulties of the poor.</u>

Student answer B

<u>Dickens' parents were imprisoned in a debtor's prison when Dickens was twelve. His father owed £40. The changes to the Poor Laws at this time meant that people who owed money would have to work to pay off their debts. The tasks they had to perform would be gruelling and tedious. It was a widely held belief that prisoners needed to think about their crimes so repetitive punishments would enable them to do this.</u>

Answer B will probably make you think, 'and your point is?' The contextual information given might be right, but it is not helpful. In fact it is all context and no comment. By contrast, the contextual information in answer A *adds* to our understanding of the novella by explaining the possible significance of a detail in the novella that might otherwise be puzzling.

A typical AQA exam-style question about how far Bob Cratchit is presented as a representative of the poor working classes might be:

AQA exam-style question

[Starting with this extract,] explore how far Dickens presents Bob Cratchit as a representative of the poor working classes in A Christmas Carol.

'Bob Cratchit as a representative of the poor working classes' is a clear focus of the question. How far he is presented as a good model of the working classes is partly a matter of *your thoughtful interpretation*. You *might* assess Bob Cratchit as a member of the poor working classes in the context of:

- expectations of the poor in Dickens' time, or even our own

- what *you* think about the poor working classes.

Using the question and the guidance, write three bullet points that you could include.

AQA points out that the best way to write usefully about contexts is:

- to make sure you answer the question

- to only include contextual information that supports a point you are making.

REVIEW IT!

1 What is the meaning of 'theme'?

2 Give three other words that mean (or roughly mean) 'responsibility'.

3 Give three other words that mean (or roughly mean) 'poverty'.

4 Give three other words that mean (or roughly mean) 'greed for money'.

5 Give three other words that mean (or roughly mean) 'celebration'.

6 In the novella, which two characters symbolise the impact of poverty on society?

7 Where does Scrooge believe the poor belong if they cannot pay their bills?

8 Dickens shows us the lavish Christmas the Lord Mayor's household enjoys. What details does he include about the servants?

9 Why does Dickens include this scene with the Lord Mayor and his Christmas preparations?

10 Here are six themes: redemption, social responsibility, Christmas, greed, poverty, family. Which two of these themes are most relevant to the following quotation?

> 'Don't be angry, Uncle. Come! Dine with us tomorrow.'

11 Here are six themes again: redemption, social responsibility, Christmas, greed, poverty, family. Which two of these themes are most relevant to the following quotation?

> 'Mankind was my business. The common welfare was my business.'

12 Give two examples in the novella of a wealthy character showing kindness.

13 Explain what The Ghost of Christmas Past means when he says:

> 'A small matter... to make these silly folks so full of gratitude.'

14 How does Scrooge defend Fezziwig to the Ghost? What does Dickens tell us about his response?

15 For each of the following, choose one quotation relevant to the theme and explain why you have chosen it.

| a | redemption | c | Christmas | e | poverty |
| b | social responsibility | d | greed | f | family |

Language, structure and form

NAILIT!

Don't be put off by Dickens' language – you can get by without understanding every word. The effort to understand it is worth it!

Language

The language of Dickens

When we talk about the language of a text, we mean how the writer *chooses* words to create effects. In other words, we are studying the writer's word *choices*. Dickens' language – although often brilliant – can be challenging for a modern reader.

Performing the text

Dickens performed his work with dramatic readings, therefore his writing is **rhythmic**, with repeated grammatical patterns. As we have seen so far in this *AQA 9 –1 GCSE English Literature Study Guide*, he also uses lists of single items or phrases. This technique helps to intensify what he's writing about, making it memorable for either his readers or the people who are listening to his dramatic reading. But he doesn't just write very long sentences: he also uses minor sentences (these are sentences without verbs, for example, 'Foggier yet, and colder! Piercing, searching, biting cold') and short sentences.

Language effects

Look at how Dickens uses layers of details in his descriptions. Scrooge and the Ghost of Christmas Present are watching a street scene where people are preparing for Christmas festivities. Here we have a description of chestnuts which uses an extended simile.

> Clauses filled with 'o' sounds make the mouth feel as if it is filled with round chestnuts.

> This dynamic verb again links to the roundness of the chestnuts as they tumble to the streets.

"
There were great, round, pot-bellied baskets of chestnuts, shaped like the waistcoats of jolly old gentlemen, lolling at the doors,
5 and tumbling out into the street in their apoplectic opulence.
"

> Notice the list describing lavish, round shapes.

> 'lolling' suggests lounging. This personification presents these chestnuts as comfortable and relaxed in their magnificence.

> This extended simile gives the reader presentation of the lavishness and splendour of Christmas as Dickens hits our senses.

This description continues with 'Cherry-cheeked apples … luscious pears', which then reappear as 'pears and apples, clustered high in blooming pyramids'. The description is framed with the repeated sentence opening of 'there were' – all overlapping one upon another to create an extravagant mountain of sumptuous food. Don't forget that for many poor people at this time, such food would not be part of their lives.

Look at how Dickens continues to **personify** this food. A 'Norfolk Biffin' is a variety of apple. By using this precise noun, Dickens immediately sets a picture of these apples in our mind. They are not just any apples; they are round, slightly flat in shape and very, very sweet:

> there were Norfolk Biffins, squab and swarthy, setting off the yellow of the oranges and lemons, and, in the great compactness of their juicy persons, urgently entreating and beseeching to be carried home in paper bags and eaten after dinner.

NAILIT!

- In your AQA exam, it is your informed response to Dickens' language that really counts.
- In your exam answer, take the time to explain why a couple of examples of Dickens' language use are effective for you. Explain what you like about them.

Consider:

- Do I like this description of the apples?
- Is it effective?
- Do I *dis*like the description in any way? If so, why? What is Dickens' intended effect? What are you supposed to think/feel towards this food?

Be honest in your answers. Many of Dickens' language choices are original, but *risky*: they do not always come off, and not everyone likes every idea – even if they like the story overall.

Dickens' use of imagery

At the start of Stave Five when Scrooge awakes and realises that he is alive and this is his chance to make changes, he announces his mood with a string of short sentences and images of himself through similes:

This weightlessness is a direct contrast to the weight of the 'flint' in the opening stave. If we think about 'light' in terms of brightness, this image also contrasts with the darkness that surrounds Scrooge in Stave One.

Would we usually associate angels with happiness? However, the 'happiness' links to the 'light' of the previous simile and the 'merry' schoolboy.

Look at how Dickens uses punctuation here. It's interesting that there's a list of three sentences separated by commas and then a full-stopped one. This creates a rhythm for reading aloud, setting the speed of the reading. It would be a slower pace if all of the sentences were punctuated by full stops.

> 'I am as light as a feather, I am as happy as an angel, I am as merry as a schoolboy. I am as giddy as a drunken man.'

This simile links to the idea of rebirth set up by an earlier metaphor, "I am quite a baby."

Notice the simplicity of these four similes in contrast to the description of Scrooge in Stave One with the extended metaphor of the cold. Scrooge has a straightforward task in front of him – he needs to accept his social responsibility.

Writing about Dickens' language in *A Christmas Carol*

Many examples of Dickens' language are worth exploring in depth. Look at this description of a London street:

> The ways were foul and narrow; the shops and houses wretched; the people half-naked, drunken, slipshod, ugly. Alleys and archways, like so many cesspools, disgorged their offences of smell, and dirt, and life, upon the straggling streets; and the whole quarter reeked with crime, with filth, and misery.

Now read one student's analysis of these words. Notice the way the student:

- refers to details in the text
- examines the *effect* and significance of the way Dickens builds this description.

Dickens immediately places the reader into a threatening and overwhelming city street. This is not a jolly street preparing for Christmas; instead it is 'foul and narrow' emphasising that this is an unwholesome environment. This pairing linked by 'and' is continued with 'shops and houses' and 'Alleys and archways', layering the sensation of being crowded by architecture. This perception continues as Dickens portrays the people as 'half-naked, drunken, slipshod, ugly', creating a sense of squalor through this choice of repellent adjectives. This use of lists continues as Dickens overwhelms the reader with the sensations 'of smell, and dirt, and life' mirroring the overpowering sensation of the 'filth' on these streets. The emotive word choices make it clear that Dickens intends the reader to feel disgust as the street 'reeks with crime'. However, the picture ends with 'misery', making the reader pause as they reconsider what may have led to this despair.

NAILIT!

In your AQA exam, analyse the effect of a couple of relevant words or phrases in the extract. This is an easy way to show you can back up your ideas with detailed textual references.

DOIT!

Choose two or three sentences from the novella that you particularly like. Explain what those sentences mean.

Analyse why Dickens' language in those sentences is effective.

Structure

NAILIT!

A recent AQA examination paper referred to the 'staves' as 'chapters'. Make sure that you are familiar with both of these terms.

A Christmas Carol is organised into five staves (chapters) that divide the **plot** into stages. It is a simple structure that is set up by the visitation of Three Spirits that form the middle section of the novella.

This is where the central conflict is at its height.

Climax

Scrooge sees the gravestone and his name.

This becomes the trigger for Scrooge to redeem himself.

The Ghost of Christmas Yet to Come shows Scrooge's future where no one cares about his death.

The Ghost of Christmas Present shows Scrooge scenes of Christmas, including some of the people who have been affected by his actions.

The Ghost of Christmas Past shows Scrooge's 'solitary' childhood. The reader begins to see why he is closed off from the world.

Marley's Ghost issues his warning.

Rising action

Exposition

Introduction to Scrooge and his world, his dislike of Christmas and lack of goodwill towards society.

Resolution

The central conflict causes a change in Scrooge. He achieves his redemption.

Parallel scenes

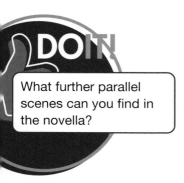

DOIT

What further parallel scenes can you find in the novella?

Dickens uses parallel scenes to draw the reader's attention to his key messages without having to **explicitly** tell them. The first key parallel is the link between Stave One and Stave Five. The plot structure here is circular, with Scrooge meeting in Stave Five the same people as in the opening scene, putting right his injustices from Stave One. Further parallel scenes are the scenes in Stave Three showing the Cratchit family Christmas and Fred's family Christmas. Although not as wealthy as Scrooge, Fred's more comfortable life is evident, unlike the poor Cratchit family. However, both of these Christmas celebrations show the generosity and goodwill of the season and provide a contrast to Scrooge's view of Christmas.

Structure and meaning

The novella's structure is *didactic* – we learn by accompanying Scrooge through his journey towards redemption. Along the way we learn about how society needs to take social responsibility for the poor.

Form

Allegory

An **allegory**, in literature, aims to teach its reader a moral or a political message. In these stories, characters are symbols of types of people in society or they represent a way of thinking. Dickens wanted to deliver a clear social message. To that end, he is able to use his character, Ebenezer Scrooge, to deliver his moral message that society must address the gap between rich and poor or face 'Doom'.

If we read the novella as an allegory, Scrooge represents cold-hearted and isolated wealthy people who see poverty as self-inflicted due to the laziness of the poor. Dickens was a vocal opponent of the Poor Laws and uses Scrooge to explore the moral position and values of those who think in this way. Scrooge represents greed, avarice and a lack of goodwill towards those who are less fortunate in society. Dickens represents this goodwill in the novella as possessing Christmas spirit.

The Christmas Ghosts can also be seen as symbolic characters. The Ghost of Christmas Past represents the power of memory in shaping the way we think and behave. The light cast on memories from the light from its head shows us how we can look at our memories and learn from them. The Ghost of Christmas Present represents charity and goodwill and the generosity shared by families and communities. The visions show how even the poorest within society or those facing harsh conditions, share the Christmas Spirit. The Ghost of Christmas Yet to Come represents the future and the death that will come to us all. Fear of death was part of Victorian life because they were surrounded by it – a lifespan was half what it is today and child mortality was high.

DO IT!

What would the Cratchit family represent in an allegory?

Victorian Gothic

By the time Dickens was writing *A Christmas Carol*, **Gothic literature** had become less fashionable; however many of the features had moved into a new form of the genre, Victorian Gothic. Dickens explores elements of this genre in his novel, *Bleak House*, by using a gloomy setting in a contemporary landscape. In *A Christmas Carol* he transfers supernatural elements of this genre into a contemporary setting where they become tangible characters equal to the other characters, rather than merely a spirit presence to trigger a fearful reaction.

REVIEW IT!

1 What does 'Humbug' mean?

2 What does 'Bah' suggest?

3 When Fred refers to 'fellow travellers' what does he mean?

4 What was 'Bedlam'?

5 When we talk about 'language' we are not talking about whether the novella is written in English or another language, so what do we mean?

6 Name two good reasons for not being put off by Dickens' language.

7 What is a simile?

8 What is a metaphor?

9 What is pathetic fallacy?

10 What does the metaphor 'a bad lobster in a dark cellar' mean?

11 What is a 'shade'?

12 What does the metaphor 'the chain I forged in life' mean?

13 What is the term for scenes that repeat or reflect other scenes?

14 When Scrooge talks to Jacob Marley he refers to Marley as 'a good man of business'. What does he mean?

15 Jacob Marley uses 'business' differently in his reply. What does he mean by 'business'?

16 At the start of Stave Two, Dickens describes Scrooge's clock as 'preposterous'. What device is he using here?

17 What does 'melancholy' mean?

18 What is 'smoking bishop'?

19 Find a place in the novella where the narrator gives their opinion. Why do you think Dickens uses this?

20 Explain how the novella's structure helps to keep the interest of the reader.

Doing well in your AQA exam

NAILIT!

In your AQA exam, the extract will come before the question, but it is a good idea to **read the question before you read the extract**. That way you will read the extract with the question focus in mind.

Understanding the question

Make sure you understand the exam question so that you do not include irrelevant material in your answer. Explore the extract *in relation to the question* rather than simply in terms of anything that grabs your attention.

The question below has been annotated by a student so that they are clear about what it is asking for.

Attitudes – what do people think and feel? How does he make us feel about money? What is he suggesting?

The extract

Dickens' methods

How to structure my response

How and why Dickens presents money – how do characters react to money? How does Dickens want us to react to it?

AQA exam-style question

Starting with this extract, explore how Dickens presents attitudes towards money in *A Christmas Carol*.

Write about:

- how Dickens presents attitudes towards money in this extract
- how Dickens presents attitudes towards money in the novella as a whole.

Might <u>we</u> react in ways that Dickens could not predict?

This student has studied the question carefully and realised that:

- the focus is on attitudes towards money
- 'present' means not just describing those attitudes but also identifying Dickens' intentions
- a modern and a Victorian reader will understand the lessons that Dickens is showing us.

'Pinning the question down' like this – making sure it is fully understood – has allowed the student to then pick out of the extract some useful evidence to support the answer.

Choose another question from earlier in this guide. Annotate the question and the extract as above.

Planning your answer

Once you have fully understood the question, planning an answer will be quite straightforward. Your brief plan should set out:

- your key, *relevant* ideas
- the content of each of four or five main paragraphs
- the order of the paragraphs.

Here is the same student's plan for their answer to the exam question on page 84:

NAILIT!

In your AQA exam, spend 10–15 minutes on understanding the question and planning your answer. There are no marks for using lots of words. Instead, you should aim to write enough *good, relevant* words. Aim for four or five well-planned paragraphs (plus a brief introduction and conclusion).

Paragraph	Content		Timing plan
1	Intro - use the question preparation to establish focus of answer		9.40
2	Explore extract - evidence of different attitudes towards money both within Scrooge and within Belle		9.43
3	How Scrooge's attitudes towards money are shown from Stave One - pay attention to language subtleties	Refer back to extract and question focus throughout. Think about what Dickens might want the reader to think reader about money.	9.58
4	How Dickens uses Scrooge's attitudes to money to convey his social message: the impact of these views on his life and on wider society, e.g. Ignorance and Want (how might a Victorian and a modern reader respond?), Marley's chain and 'torment'.		10.06
5	How Dickens presents the positive use of money: the happiness Fezziwig brings with just a little money; Fred's kindness and help to the Cratchit family; Scrooge stopping the death of the 'Christ' figure, Tiny Tim.		10.14
6	Conclusion - brief return to question/are these lessons relevant today?		10.22

Sticking to the plan

Note how this student has jotted down time points when they should move on to the next section of their answer. That way they make sure they do not get stuck on one point and fail to cover the question focus in enough breadth.

Planning to meet the mark scheme

The plan above suggests that the student has thought carefully about the focus of the question, that they are familiar with the mark scheme for their AQA 19th-century novel question and are planning to cover its requirements. (See the summary mark scheme on page 86.)

DOIT!

Go back to the exam question that you chose for the Do it! on page 76. Develop a brief plan for it as above.

Assessment objective (AO)	What the plan promises
AO1 Read, understand and respond	Understanding of a number of ideas relevant to the main question focus – how positive and negative attitudes towards money are shown by Dickens and the impact of these attitudes on characters and on society. Some personal interpretations to be included – suggested by consideration of how attitudes towards money might be relevant to our society.
AO2 Language, form and structure	Exploring extract will ensure close engagement with Dickens' language. Annotations already point to this.
AO3 Contexts	Consideration of: how modern readers might view these attitudes to money and what Dickens intended his contemporary readers to learn and understand.

What your AQA examiner is looking for

Your AQA examiner will mark your answer according to a mark scheme based on three assessment objectives (AOs). The AOs focus on specific knowledge, understanding and skills. Together, they are worth 30 marks, so it is important to understand what the examiner is looking out for.

Mark scheme

Your AQA examiner will mark your answers in 'bands'. These bands roughly equate as follows:

- band 6 approx. grades 8 and 9
- band 5 approx. grades 6 and 7
- band 4 approx. grades 5 and 6
- band 3 approx. grades 3 and 4
- band 2 approx. grades 1 and 2.

Most importantly, the improvement descriptors in the table below – based on the AQA mark scheme – will help you understand how to improve your answers and gain more marks. The maximum number of marks for each AO is shown.

Assessment objective (AO)		Improvement descriptors				
		Band 2 Your answer…	Band 3 Your answer…	Band 4 Your answer…	Band 5 Your answer…	Band 6 Your answer…
AO1 12 marks	Read, understand and respond	is relevant and backs up ideas with references to the novella.	sometimes explains the novella in relation to the question.	clearly explains the novella in relation to the question.	thoughtfully explains the novella in relation to the question.	critically explores the novella in relation to the question.
	Use evidence	makes some comments about these references.	refers to details in the novella to back up points.	carefully chooses close references to the novella to back up points.	thoughtfully builds appropriate references into points.	chooses precise details from the novella to make points convincing.
AO2 12 marks	Language, form and structure	mentions some of Dickens' methods.	comments on some of Dickens' methods, and their effects.	clearly explains Dickens' key methods, and their effects.	thoughtfully explores Dickens' methods, and their effects.	analyses Dickens' methods, and how these influence the reader.
	Subject terminology	uses some subject terminology.	uses some relevant terminology.	helpfully uses varied, relevant terminology.	makes thoughtful use of relevant terminology.	chooses subject terminology to make points precise and convincing.
AO3 6 marks	Contexts	makes some simple **inferences** about contexts.	infers Dickens' point of view and the significance of contexts.	shows a clear appreciation of Dickens' point of view and the significance of contexts.	explores Dickens' point of view and the significance of relevant contexts.	makes perceptive and revealing links between the novella and relevant contexts.

AO1 Read, understand and respond/Use evidence

Make sure you read and answer the question carefully and thoughtfully. The examiner will be looking out for evidence that you have answered the question. Do not make the mistake of going into your exam with an answer in mind: you must concentrate on the aspect that the question focuses on. Knowing the novella well will give you the confidence to do that.

'Use evidence' means helpful references to the novella. These references can be indirect references – brief mentions of an event or what a character says or does – or direct references – quotations. Choose and use evidence carefully so that it clearly supports a point you are making. Quotations should be as short as possible, and the very best ones are often neatly built into your own writing.

AO2 Language, form and structure/Subject terminology

The characters in *A Christmas Carol* are not real people; they have been *created* by Dickens to entertain and influence the audience. Good answers will explore how Dickens chooses language to create characters and situations, and to have effects on the reader.

Subject terminology is about choosing your words carefully, using the right words and avoiding vague expressions. It is also about using terminology *helpfully*. For example, here are two different uses of subject terminology, the first much more useful than the second:

> ### Student answer A
> Dickens introduces Scrooge by describing him with a long list of non-finite verbs: 'A squeezing, wrenching, grasping, scraping...' The use of this list suggests that these unlikeable characteristics are limitless and infinite. Dickens lets the reader know immediately that we are not supposed to like Scrooge.

> ### Student answer B
> 'Squeezing' is a non-finite verb.

AO3 Contexts

Notice the emphasis on '*relevant* contexts' higher up the mark criteria. The best answers will include contextual information that is directly relevant to the *question*, not just the novella. (See answer A on page 68 for a good example.) Consider how might:

- the society Dickens lived in have influenced his ideas and attitudes?

- the society *you* live in influence how *you* respond to ideas and attitudes in the novella?

- knowledge of the whole novella enrich your understanding of the extract?

AO4: Vocabulary, sentence structures, spelling and punctuation

Make sure that you use a range of vocabulary and sentence structures for clarity, purpose and effect. Accurate spelling and punctuation is important too for this assessment objective.

NAILIT!

To boost your marks, when answering questions do the following:

- Know the novella well. Read it and study it.

- Don't go into your exam with ready-prepared answers.

- Read the question and make sure you answer it thoughtfully.

- Choose details from the novella that will support your points.

- Don't treat the novella and its characters as though they are real. Instead ask why Dickens has chosen to create a particular **dialogue** or event. What effect is he trying to achieve?

NAILIT!

Introductions and conclusions need to be useful or they simply waste time. Your opening:

- should be short and relevant
- could introduce a particular angle on the question, or interpretation
- could answer the question directly (leaving the rest of the answer to provide supporting detail).

Writing your answer

Getting started

Here are the openings of two students' answers to the question we have already looked at on page 84:

> **Student answer A**
>
> Dickens presents attitudes to money as complex, varied and frequently divisive. In this extract from Stave Two, Dickens shows his wealth-conscious Victorian readers how prioritising money can lose you more important sources of happiness, like love, as Belle sadly breaks off her engagement with Scrooge because he has become too driven by wealth and they have grown apart.

> **Student answer B**
>
> I am going to write about attitudes to money and how they are different between different people in the novella. Scrooge is really mean. Fred is kind and generous and he keeps inviting his uncle to dinner. Those are the sorts of things I'm going to write about in my answer about *A Christmas Carol* in answer to the exam question about...

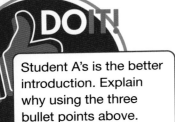

DOIT!

Student A's is the better introduction. Explain why using the three bullet points above.

The extract

You do not need to write about the extract and *then* about the rest of the play. You *can* compare the extract with other parts of the play throughout your answer. However, a safe approach – just to make sure you do give the extract enough attention – is to begin with the extract and then make connections with other parts of the play in the following paragraphs. This is the approach suggested in the plan you have already looked at.

Here is part of that student's third paragraph. Note how they closely examine relevant details of Dickens' language choices. An examiner has made some comments in the margin.

> From the start of Stave One, Scrooge's attitudes to money are established as 'tight-fisted' and 'grasping'. These images of hands tensely 'squeezing' as they seek money links with Dickens' description of Scrooge as a 'covetous sinner'. The adjective, 'Covetous' shows Scrooge's greedy quest for money. This 'covetous' nature connected to 'sinner' shows how his love of money is central to his need for redemption and foreshadows the warning from Jacob Marley.

Good topic sentence setting out a clear point that is referenced to wording in the exam question.

Direct evidence used well – built neatly into student's own words.

Effect of words is identified.

Precise and useful terminology.

Paragraph topics

Each of your paragraphs should deal with a subtopic of the main focus of the question. The plan for the question about money (page 84) suggests that the next three paragraph topics will be, how Dickens: uses Scrooge's attitudes to money to convey his social message; presents the positive effects of wealth and how that can benefit society; whether these messages still relevant today. This last paragraph will help the student to directly consider the 'how Dickens presents' aspect of the question: they will have to consider what Dickens is trying to suggest via the contrasts between attitudes towards money.

Below you will see how – in this 'how Dickens…to convey his social message' paragraph – the same student makes references back to both the extract and the question so as to stay sharply relevant. The references are underlined to point them out.

> Dickens demonstrates how Scrooge's attitude towards money has become more powerful than his love for Belle when she claims 'another idol' has 'displaced' her, implying that like many wealthy Victorians, Scrooge seems to have let money guide his decisions for most of his adult life, and suggests he worships and values money as he once valued her. This attitude towards money is presented as toxic, causing Scrooge to cut himself off from the warmth of human relationships, leaving him carrying 'his own low temperature' with him as he remains cut off from society. This isolation, like that of wealthy Victorians, leads to the creation of 'Ignorance and Want', the two 'hideous' children created by 'Man's' failure to face the effects of poverty and deprivation on the most vulnerable members of society. Here the reader sees a physical manifestation of Scrooge's attitudes towards money - and this manifestation will bring 'Doom' to society.

Using evidence:

This student makes their points using precise terminology, direct evidence in the form of quotations, as well as indirect evidence when referring to another part of the text. Both forms of evidence are valid, but do quote from the extract at least – if only to show you can handle quotations.

Ending your answer

If you write a conclusion, make it useful: don't simply repeat what you have already said. The answer we have been looking at ends by summarising the student's personal response:

> On balance I think that Dickens presents Scrooge as cut off from society through his avarice and love of money. His attitude leads to the loss of love from Belle, who he really cared for. The reader sees that it is his attitude towards money that causes his need for redemption, but why does Dickens make that redemption so easy and cost so little money for Scrooge?

This conclusion adds little to the student's answer. It merely re-states their overall point. The last sentence raises an interesting question, but it would have been better placed in an earlier paragraph where it could have been briefly explored.

DO IT!

Use the preparation and planning you did for your chosen exam question (see page 84) to write a full answer.

STRETCH IT!

Develop a range of evaluative vocabulary to enable you to pinpoint Dickens' intention. Use words like: 'condemns', 'criticises', 'exposes', 'ridicules', 'subverts', 'questions'.

Going for the top grades

Of course you will always try to write the best answer possible, but if you are aiming for the top grades then it is vital to be clear about what examiners will be looking out for. The best answers will tend to:

• develop a conceptual response to the exam question • show insight into the novella and the question focus by developing a clear argument • explore meaning in the novella in relation to the focus of the question • choose and use evidence precisely and wisely	**AO1**
• analyse Dickens' methods and their effect on the reader • use relevant, helpful subject terminology	**AO2**
• explore aspects of context that are relevant to the novella and the question.	**AO3**

Conceptual response

A conceptual response means establishing a particular 'angle' on the question focus, and using that angle as a reference point for the whole answer.

The best answers will be RIPE with ideas and engagement:

R	Relevant	Stay strictly relevant to the question.
I	Insightful	Develop relevant insights into the play, its characters, themes and dramatic techniques.
P	Precise	Choose and use evidence precisely so that it strengthens your points.
E	Exploratory	Explore relevant aspects of the play, looking at it from more than one angle.

Below is part of a student's answer to the question: how does Dickens present the theme of redemption in *A Christmas Carol*? The student is developing the challenging idea that Dickens presents some aspects of Scrooge's actions in a positive light. Next to the answer are some comments by an examiner.

DO IT!

Find an essay or practice answer you have written about *A Christmas Carol*.

Use the advice and examples on this page to help you decide how your writing could be improved.

Even at his worst in Stave One, Scrooge might have shown some glimmers that he might have been ripe and ready for redemption that a Victorian reader would have recognised. Scrooge might display all of the miserly behaviours that would make him a 'covetous sinner', but his sarcastic word-play ('buried with a stake of holly through his heart') shows some ability to connect with the world around him, inspiring his nephew Fred to repeatedly ask him to 'dine with us tomorrow.' Scrooge's instinct is to cut himself off from the 'Humbug' of Christmas, with the excesses of spending, especially those who are 'poor enough'. Perhaps we should see Scrooge's appeal to Fred to 'Let me keep it my own way' as a way of spending Christmas without meaning that you will have to pay 'bills without money'. So maybe this level-headed attitude towards Christmas could be seen as his nod to redemption...

Original insight related to context.

Complexities of Scrooge's behaviour introduced here.

Precise evidence neatly integrated into argument.

Tentatively introduced insight/ hypothesis

Good return to question focus to maintain relevance.

REVIEW IT!

1 What should you do before you read the extract from the novella?

2 Why should you do that before reading the extract?

3 How long should you spend on understanding the question and planning the answer?

4 What three things should be covered in your plan?

5 Why is it helpful to build timings into your plan?

6 How many paragraphs is a good number to plan for?

7 Why is it useful to know the mark scheme?

8 Should you write an introduction and a conclusion?

9 Do you have to write about the extract before writing about the rest of the novella?

10 What should each paragraph of your answer be about?

11 Must you quote from the extract?

12 What is meant by 'evidence'?

13 What should be the focus of your revision in the final month?

14 It is vital that your answer is relevant. Relevant to what?

15 What four ideas should be kept in mind when trying to write a top grade answer?

16 Why is this a bad conclusion to an answer?

> So that is what I think - Scrooge is able to find redemption at the end of the novella. I think I've made it clear why

17 Why is this a slightly better conclusion?

> Dickens presents Scrooge's redemption as key to *A Christmas Carol*, as he draws attention to the ill-treatment of the poor in the Victorian era and provides a message of hope for the future through the transformation of the cold, miserly, bitter character of Ebenezer Scrooge, into a warm, charitable philanthropist who epitomises Christmas spirit.

18 Here is an AQA exam-style question:

AQA exam-style question

[Starting with this extract,] explore how Dickens presents the supernatural in *A Christmas Carol*.

Annotate the question to help you understand it fully.

19 Write a plan for an answer to the question above.

20 Write one main paragraph that you have planned for.

NAIL IT!

In the month leading up to the exam, all your revision should be based on planning and writing answers to exam questions. You will find plenty of AQA exam-style questions in this *GCSE 9–1 AQA English Literature Study Guide*.

AQA exam-style questions

On these pages you will find two practice questions for *A Christmas Carol*. In your exam you will only get one question: you will not have a choice of questions. Self-assessment guidance is provided on the app/online.

PRACTICE QUESTION 1

NAILIT!

- The question comes immediately after the extract.
- Read the question first.
- Make sure you read the extract with the question in mind.

Read the following extract from Stave One of *A Christmas Carol* and then answer the question that follows.

At this point in the novella, it is Christmas Eve and Scrooge is closing the counting house. Scrooge is talking to the clerk, Bob Cratchit.

At length the hour of shutting up the counting-house arrived. With an ill will Scrooge dismounted from his stool, and tacitly admitted the fact to the expectant clerk in the tank, who instantly snuffed his candle out, and put on his hat.

5 'You'll want all day to-morrow, I suppose?' said Scrooge.

'If quite convenient, sir.'

'It's not convenient,' said Scrooge, 'and it's not fair. If I was to stop half a crown for it, you'd think yourself ill-used, I'll be bound?'

The clerk smiled faintly.

10 'And yet,' said Scrooge, 'you don't think me ill-used, when I pay a day's wages for no work.'

The clerk observed that it was only once a year.

'A poor excuse for picking a man's pocket every twenty-fifth of December!' said Scrooge, buttoning his great-coat to the chin. 'But I suppose you must

15 have the whole day. Be here all the earlier next morning.'

The clerk promised that he would; and Scrooge walked out with a growl. The office was closed in a twinkling, and the clerk, with the long ends of his white comforter dangling below his waist (for he boasted no great-coat), went down a slide on Cornhill, at the end of a lane of boys, twenty times, in

20 honour of its being Christmas Eve, and then ran home to Camden Town as hard as he could pelt, to play at blindman's-buff.

Starting with this extract, explore how Dickens presents the world of work in *A Christmas Carol*.

Write about:

- how Dickens presents the world of work in this extract
- how Dickens presents the world of work in the novella as a whole.

[30 marks]

PRACTICE QUESTION 2

Read this extract from Stave Three of *A Christmas Carol* and then answer the question that follows.

Scrooge is with the Ghost of Christmas Present. He is watching a scene from Fred's Christmas party.

Scrooge's nephew revelled in another laugh, and as it was impossible to keep the infection off, though the plump sister tried hard to do it with aromatic vinegar, his example was unanimously followed.

5 'I was only going to say,' said Scrooge's nephew, 'that the consequence of his taking a dislike to us, and not making merry with us, is, as I think, that he loses some pleasant moments, which could do him no harm. I am sure he loses pleasanter companions than he can find in his own thoughts, either in his mouldy old office, or his
10 dusty chambers. I mean to give him the same chance every year, whether he likes it or not, for I pity him. He may rail at Christmas till he dies, but he can't help thinking better of it – I defy him – if he finds me going there in good temper, year after year, and saying "Uncle Scrooge, how are you?" If it only puts him in the vein to leave
15 his poor clerk fifty pounds, *that's* something; and I think I shook him yesterday.'

It was their turn to laugh now at the notion of his shaking Scrooge. But, being thoroughly good-natured, and not much caring what they laughed at, so that they laughed at any rate, he encouraged them in
20 their merriment, and passed the bottle, joyously.

Starting with this extract, explore how Dickens presents the character of Fred, Scrooge's nephew, in *A Christmas Carol*.

Write about:

- how Dickens presents the character of Fred in this extract

- how Dickens presents the character of Fred in the novella as a whole

[30 marks]

Glossary

allegory A narrative (or image) that can be interpreted to reveal a hidden meaning. This meaning is usually a moral or political lesson.

alliteration Words starting with the same sound that the writer has placed near each other for **effect** (for example: the big, blue bus; one kick caused chaos).

charactonym A name, especially for a fictional character, that suggests a distinctive feature of that character (for example: *Mistress Quickly*).

connotation The implied (see **implicit** also) meaning of a word or phrase. For example, the word *mob* means a large group of people, but it *connotes* violence. If someone *dashes* down the road, we know that they are moving quickly, but that choice of word also connotes urgency. A connotation is sometimes called a nuance.

context The context of a poem, play, novel or story is the set of conditions in which it was written. These might include: the writer's life; society, habits and beliefs at the time they wrote; an event that influenced the writing; and the genre of the writing. The context is also seen in terms of influences on the reader, so for example, a modern audience would see a Dickens novel differently from audiences in his own time, as their life experiences would be different.

dialogue The words that characters say in plays or in **fiction**. In fiction, these words are usually shown within inverted commas ('…').

dramatic irony When the reader has information that a character in a story does not.

effect The impact of a writer's words on a reader: how the words create a mood, feeling or reaction.

emotive language Words chosen to make a reader feel a particular way about something (for example: *Poor*, *hungry*, *little mites* or *Great, hulking bullies*).

evidence Details or clues that support a **point of view**. A quotation can be a form of evidence in which a few words are copied from a text to support a point of view.

explicit Explicit information is clearly stated; it's on the surface of a text and should be obvious.

fiction Novels or stories made up by an author.

foil A character that provides a contrast with another character, often to show their good qualities.

Gothic literature A genre of literature and film that combines **fiction** and horror, death, and at times romance. See **fiction**.

imagery The 'pictures' a writer puts into the reader's mind. **Similes** and **metaphors** are particular forms of imagery. We also talk about violent, graphic or religious imagery, and so on.

implicit (imply) Implicit information is only suggested (or implied), it is not stated directly; we have to **infer** to understand it. The opposite of **explicit**.

infer (inference) To 'read between the lines'; to work out meaning from clues in the text. See **implicit**. When we infer, we are making an inference.

interpret To work out meaning, using clues and **evidence**. The same piece of writing can be interpreted in different ways, but evidence has to support interpretations.

intrusive (narration) Where the **narrator** speaks directly to the reader, comments on what is happening and can be seen as another character.

irony In literature, irony arises when the reality of a situation is different to how it may appear or what expectations may be.

language (choices) The words and the **style** that a writer chooses in order to have an **effect** on a reader.

limited omniscient narrator A **narrator** who knows what one character is thinking and feeling and can comment to the reader about this, but who cannot see inside any of the other characters' heads.

metaphor Comparing two things by referring to them as though they are the same thing (for example: His face *was a thunder cloud*. The boy *was an angry bear*).

motif Something with a symbolic meaning that is repeated throughout a text to establish a theme or a certain mood. A motif can be almost anything (for example: an idea, an object, a concept, a character type, the weather).

narrator The person who tells the story. A *first person narrator* tells the story as though it is happening to them personally (for example: *I* walked slowly down the street). A *third person narrator* tells the story from someone else's point of view (for example: *He* walked slowly down the street).

noun phrase A group of words that contains a noun and acts as the subject or object of a sentence (for example: *old county family.*)

pathetic fallacy This is where nature (for example: weather) is used to reflect human emotions.

personification (personify) A **metaphor** that represents a thing as a living creature (for example: the waves were *leaping white horses*. The storm *threatened* the town).

phrase A group of words that do a job together in a sentence (for example: he looked *under the bed*).

plot The plot of a literary text is the *story* – the narrative – or an interrelated series of events as described by the author.

point of view See **viewpoint**.

quotation A word, **phrase**, sentence or passage copied from a text, usually used to support an argument or **point of view**. A quotation should be surrounded by inverted commas ('…'). It is usually wise to make quotations as short as possible, sometimes just one well-chosen word is enough.

rhythm (rhythmic) The 'beat' in prose, poetry or music.

setting The setting is the *time and place* in which a play or story takes place. The setting could also include the social and political circumstances (or **context**) of the action.

simile Comparing two things using either the word *like* or *as* (for example: The boy was *like an angry bear*. His running was *as loud as thunder*. Her face was *as yellow as custard*).

stave A verse of a song.

structure How a text is organised and held together: all those things that shape a text and make it coherent.

style Writing styles can vary between writers, or writers may use different styles at different times (for example: they might sometimes write informally with energy, while in other texts they might write formally, creating a style that gives them an air of authority). Style and **tone** are closely related.

technique Another word for method. Writers use different techniques to create different **effects**.

theme A theme is a central idea in a text. Common themes in novels, films, poems and other literary texts include: loyalty, love, race, betrayal, poverty, good versus evil, and so on.

tone The mood of a text, or the attitude of the author or **narrator** towards the topic. Tones can be mocking, affectionate, polite, authoritative, and so on.

viewpoint A writer's or character's point of view: their attitudes, beliefs and opinions.

vocabulary The words a writer chooses to use. They might use a particular sort of vocabulary (for example: formal, simple or shocking).

voice (narrative) A written account of connected events can be neutral in opinion. Sometimes a writer's attitude and **tone** is much more noticeable – as though you can 'hear' them. This is the writer's voice.